DAVID MUNCASTER

Theatre has been part of David's life ever since his school days. He is on record for saying that drama studies were just about the only thing he was any good at, but turned down an opportunity to work at the Nottingham Playhouse as an Assistant Stage Manager because the cost of rent, food and bus fare were greater than the salary on offer. Instead he immersed himself into amateur theatre where he has done everything with the exception of prompt; which he wouldn't do "for all the tea in China"!

He began writing as a teenager, firstly lyrics for a rock band then articles for a student magazine before starting work on his first book. It took a surprising long time before David finally combined his passion for theatre with writing but his first play, *Call Girls* was an immediate success being published by New Theatre Publications and having performances in both the UK and the USA. Since then there have been hundreds of performances of David's work around the world by both amateur and professional companies with his festival friendly one act plays regularly winning awards.

In 2010 he answered an advertisement in *Amateur Stage* for a playscript reviewer and with an average of eight plays a month his reviews have become one of the most popular features in the magazine.

David lives in Cheshire where he is an active participant for two amateur groups and an enthusiastic supporter of all forms of theatre.

www.davidmuncaster.com

THE PLAY'S THE THING

David Muncaster

Playscript reviews published in
Amateur Stage Magazine 2010-2011

SILVERMOON PUBLISHING
London
www.silvermoonpublishing.co.uk

THE PLAY'S THE THING

First published in Great Britain in December 2013
by Silvermoon Publishing
3rd Floor, 207 Regent Street, London, W1B 3HH

Typeset by Douglas Mayo

A CIP catalogue record for this book is available from the British
Library.

ISBN 978 1 840 94943 8

For Margaret

Contents

CONTENTS

CONTENTS

INTRODUCTION

Writing has been part of my life for as long as I can remember. When I was a teenager and my school friends went off to colleges and university I would keep in touch by writing letters in story form, often featuring a disreputable character called Fred, who's adventures added a bit of glamour to the otherwise mundane recounting of episodes from real life.

At around this time I joined a band for which I came up with the name of Strauss. We played blues based music and the name was supposed to refer to the jeans manufacturer Levi Strauss but so many people associated the name with classical music we eventually caved in and started playing *The Blue Danube* as part of our set. Playing blues based music around the pubs of Nottingham at a time when Punk Rock was all the rage, the band were never destined for the big time but, as resident lyricist, I started to realise that writing was something I really enjoyed.

It wasn't long before I took the saying "everyone has a book in them" to heart and began work on my magnum opus! I wonder how many writers never actually complete anything because they get bogged down trying to write a great novel? I knew what I wanted to write about and I had my characters but I was stuck in a rut for years because, whenever I felt like writing, I thought I had better try to do a bit of my novel. It was a millstone around my neck and it never really got off the ground despite the amount of time I spent on it because every time I read what I had previously written I felt it wasn't good enough. It was a great relief when I finally plucked up the courage to throw the whole thing in the bin and forget I had ever started it!

I then revived my interest in theatre. Drama was the only thing that I was actually any good at when I was at school and I very nearly began a career in theatre as an assistant stage manager with the Nottingham Playhouse before deciding to take a less interesting, but better paid job, outside of the world of theatre. My renewed interest came about due, in part, to the privatisation of the railway industry. My job in Nottingham ceased to exist and I moved to the North West to take up a new role. Not knowing anyone in the area, I thought that an excellent way to meet new people would be to join my local amateur dramatics group. Soon I was acting and directing and loving every moment.

Having found a new outlet for my creative side it was only a matter of time before I wrote his first play and I was surprised at how easily it came. I chose a situation with which I was familiar and created characters that seemed real to me. Within one evening I had written my fist short play. This was *Call Girls*, about people working in a call centre (before you get the wrong impression), and has been published by New Theatre Publications. I was bowled over by the whole thing. Having spent about fifteen years trying and failing to write a novel, within a couple of months of deciding to write a play, I was a published author!

I soon discovered that being published and being performed are two very different things so, whilst waiting for Cameron Mackintosh to take notice of my little play I sent another, *Waiting for a Train*, a rather serious piece about the casual use of cannabis and the link to schizophrenia, off to a play competition in Chicago. This was selected for a rehearsed reading and was the first time something I had written (other than song lyrics) had been performed in front of an audience. Next came some very short plays performed in the Gone in Sixty Seconds Festival then, in 2009, I won the Congleton One Act Play Festival with *Mission Impossible*, a satire about corporate life. This win gave me a lot of satisfaction: the entries for this festival came from all over the world and were 'blind read' by a panel meaning that they knew nothing of the author when they chose the plays that would be performed. It was pure coincidence that one of the authors chosen, me, lived just down the road! On the night of the festival the overall winner was chosen by audience vote and I was dragged on to the stage to receive my prize.

More plays followed and, although I don't expect that I'll ever get rich on the royalties, I do get a little thrill every time I receive a performance notification to know that somewhere in the world someone is going to be watching one of my plays.

Theatre is now a passion and I see as much live theatre, both amateur and professional, as I can. I always maintain that the only difference between amateur and professional actors is how they earn the money to pay their mortgages and some of the best productions I have witnessed have been on the amateur stage.

When the opportunity to review scripts for Amateur Stage magazine came along I grabbed it with both hands. I love the huge variety of scripts that pop through my letter box and, because I am writing reviews, it means that I read plays that would normally pass me by. This is where I have made the greatest discoveries: I remember expecting to hate *It Felt Empty When the Heart Went At First But It Is Alright Now* when I picked up the script but I was overwhelmed by the quality of the writing and the author, Lucy Kirkwood, is a huge talent who, I am sure, will arouse and and excite audiences for many years to come.

I am very aware that my reviews are only my opinion and are, necessarily, subjective. However, the same is true of any review and I feel that I do have the experience and background to at least be fair when I praise or criticise. When I love a play the review writes itself but the most difficult reviews to write are where I am not moved either way. Thankfully, they are few and far between.

There is nothing like live theatre and with both new and established writers consistently supplying the medium with fresh work the future is assured. I hope that these reviews prove useful and if they lead to a director choosing a play that they might not have done otherwise then I will be very satisfied.

David Muncaster
December 2013

Reviews
2010 - 2011

ABOUT DOG
Author: Shannon Murdoch
Publisher: www.productionscripts.com
ISBN NO: None
Cast: 1M 1F
Type: Full length

About Dog is the story of two disturbed people. Nell is a woman worried by ghosts; Owen a visitor who seems to be a participant in her nightmares. I wasn't entirely sure whether the dog of the title was real or imaginary. In fact I wondered if the dog was Nell, Owen or all of the above, such is the Aburdist nature of the play.

At first, Nell, troubled though she is, exercises control over Owen. Then the balance of power shifts as the play develops and I started to wonder if we were heading for a happy ending but, in the end, I wasn't really sure of anything. Having finished the script, I read the synopsis and it all made a bit more sense but I don't feel that the play conveys the story clearly enough to hold one's attention.

AS WE FORGIVE THOSE
Author: Andrew Smith
Publisher: Samuel French
ISBN NO: 9780573132063
Cast: 3F
Type: One Act

Alex, a girl in her late teens, sits in her sister's living room. Sophie, the sister, comes home from work and is shocked to see her: "How did you get in?" she demands. It seems that Alex has broken in through a window and she pleads with her sister not to call the police. She needs help; somewhere to stay. Eventually Sophie agrees but it is clear that there is something very much amiss with the siblings' relationship.

The sisters are very different: Alex survives on the streets, hangs around with gangs and mugs people to make ends meet; Sophie is a Christian, successful in her chosen profession and attractive – apart from a scar on her cheek.

Sophie's flatmate, Jen, comes home, sees Alex, and is convinced that she is the girl who mugged her and stole her mobile phone. Alex, of course, denies it all, but she is soon found out.

As We Forgive Those explores the bonds that exist between family and friends with Sophie choosing to stand by her sister despite the permanent reminder that she carries on her face of how Alex has behaved in the past. It is written with a teenage audience in mind but says nothing new.

BEAUTY AND THE BEAST
Author: Bob Bishop
Publisher: Spotlight Publications
ISBN NO: 9781907307263
Cast: 7M 4F + extras
Type: Pantomime

Gilbert Cornwallis is a wealthy merchant who has gambled and lost everything he owns with the exception of the barrel he stands up in and a locket. Deciding that he must sell the latter he leaves his daughters Patience, Charity and Beauty and sets off to London, stopping on the way to rest at Castle Beastly. There he steals a rose to take home to Beauty but he is caught by the fearsome Beast who demands that Gilbert brings him a hostage of the first living creature to greet him when he gets home. I wonder who that might be!

The story is narrated by a minstrel who sings, dances and strums the lute. The knockabouts, Willy and Wally, consider themselves to be notorious villains but live in fear of the dame. The principal boy is Simon and, though described as handsome and vain, the author takes care to point out that he and all the other characters have their good qualities. Patience and Charity are not ugly sisters but quite normal compared to Beauty's over-the-top sweetness, whilst the Dame is not a battleaxe but a kindly widow who has softness and affection for Gilbert.

It is quite a long script and I wonder if little ones might become restless before we reach the happy ending ut with plenty of music, laughter and jokes old and new Beauty and the Beast has everything required of a pantomime.

18

BLACKOUT
Author: Davey Anderson
Publisher: Samuel French
ISBN NO: 9780573052583
Cast: Variable
Type: Short play

Blackout is a short play that was first performed as part of the New Connections programme at the National Theatre. It can be presented as a monologue or with a cast of up to twelve people.

Based on a true story, the play is the tale of James, a fifteen year old Glaswegian who has committed a violent crime. It describes his growing up, being a bit of an outsider, his fascination with the far right and his love for his grandfather. A cocktail of drugs and alcohol leads to James committing an act that he can barely remember and he is expecting a long custodial sentence.

If all this sounds a bit grim, then please be assured that it is not the case. Despite everything, James is a likeable character and the play has an upbeat ending.

I believe that Blackout would be best presented as a monologue and I would expect it to resonate with a teenage audience.

BOTH SIDES
Author: Sue Welch
Publisher: J Garnett Miller
ISBN NO: 97808533436775
Cast: 3M 3F
Type: One Act

Bill's marriage has broken down after fourteen years. His wife, Louise, now has a new boyfriend and, six months after moving out of the family home, Bill has turned to a counsellor for help. Meanwhile, Louise's boyfriend wants to move in and, whilst she is not sure whether this is a good idea, her sister is very enthusiastic; almost too enthusiastic. Eventually we learn that the sister's hatred of Bill stems from jealousy, she wanted Bill for herself, and she is doing her best to be supportive now.

The counsellor is a quite an odd character. He doesn't seem to have much in the way of counselling skills and has a total lack of empathy: at one point he even admonishes his client for using a mild swear word. I cannot imagine that happening in a real counselling session but all becomes clear with a surprising twist at the end.

This is quite a neat little one act play but it is let down by lack of defined characters. Bill is angry, Louise vacillates and their daughter is sulky but I didn't feel that I really got to know any of them which resulted in my not being as moved by the ending as I should have been.

BUNNY
Author: Jack Thorne
Publisher: Nick Hern Books
ISBN NO: 9781848421349
Cast: 1F

Katie is eighteen and still at school. She plays the clarinet, badly, in the school orchestra and has Guardian-reading parents of the type that would, and did, march their daughter back to shops, where she'd done a bit of shoplifting, to return the goods and ask the shopkeeper if they wanted to press charges. Katie has an older boyfriend, Abe. He works at Vauxhall in the offices but prefers the people who work in the factory. Abe is black. That doesn't matter in a middle-class oh-that-doesn't-matter kind of way.

Katie tells the story as a monologue. Abe has waited for her to finish orchestra practice and is walking her home from school when a kid on a bike knocks Abe's ice cream from his hand. There is a fight, which Abe considers himself to have won, but when two pals who have seen the fight stop their car, the testosterone levels rise alarmingly. They chase after the kid and find the address but when they get there Asif, the driver, sends Abe and the other man away so that Katie is alone in the car with him. Katie insists that she is in control: she knows what she is doing, but the fact that Asif is just teasing her, gets her to expose herself and then rejects her, proves that that she is out of her depth.

The play has humour: Katie's peculiar dereliction is to restrict her shoplifting to cleaning products, "I could nick them J-cloths and no would notice", but its strength is the insight into the agonies of coming-of-age. Shortly after Katie's humiliation she finds herself in a position of power over the kid on the bike and revenge is hers.

Bunny is a rousing drama that is bound to appeal to lovers of TV programmes such as Shameless and Skins.

CAFÉ BROSSE
Author: Jean McConnell
Publisher: Samuel French
ISBN NO: 9780573115424
Cast: 3M 3F 2 Other

George and Seraphine are an English couple who, for the last fifteen years, have run the Café Brosse in rural France. The trouble is that Seraphine has had enough: Enough of France, enough of the Café Brosse and, most particularly, enough of George.

What can a man do? This is the question that George puts to his best friend, Aramis, who has the answer ready: if a man's wife is unhappy, discontented, dissatisfied and restless, the best thing a man can do is to have an affair! The thing is that George is already having an affair; it has been going on for the last five years. Seraphine knows all about it and she approves. So, Aramis has another suggestion: why don't Seraphine and George's mistress swap places?

Jean McConnell has written more than two dozen stage plays, including the immensely popular 'Deckchairs' series, in a career lasting fifty years. Her experience shows in the creation of a set of engaging characters and a plot that chugs along nicely enough. Audiences will probably see the end coming but it is of no matter. Café Brosse is a classic style comedy that should afford them a pleasant, if not especially memorable, evening's entertainment.

CALENDAR GIRLS
Author: Tim Firth
Publisher: Samuel French
ISBN NO: 9780573110672
Cast: 4M 10F

Tim Firth is responsible for one of my own more memorable experiences in theatre. Some years ago I played Gordon in an amateur production of Neville's Island. At the end of one evening the Front of House Manager informed me that a couple had walked out during the interval vowing never to return to that particular theatre again. When she enquired what had angered them they replied, 'That Gordon!' Well at least it wasn't the acting. I cannot see Calendar Girls causing such offence, even allowing for that one thing that everyone knows about this play.

The nudity is brief and hidden from the audience but, all the same, any society planning to put this on will need to ensure that they have a game bunch of girls in their number as well as a theatre that is free from draughts. Well, they will once this play becomes available for amateur production: it is not possible to obtain a licence at present, though that fact has not harmed sales of the script.

The play is, of course, based on the true story of a group of ladies from a Women's Institute in Yorkshire who created a nude calendar to raise money for leukaemia research. As the action starts we are in Knapeley Church Hall where Cora is belting out 'Jerusalem' which is doing nothing to enhance the atmosphere of 'Eastern Mysticism' that Chris is attempting to enjoy as part of her t'ai chi class. Time passes and the girls celebrate each new season in their own unique way. As Chris wryly points out, 'If more people did WI, there'd be half the need for hallucinogenic drugs'.

There are plenty of laughs but amongst them are huge dollops of pathos. Anne's husband, John, has 'got his results,' as the play begins and with the passing of time his treatment intensifies and his condition worsens. Anne's visits to Skipton Hospital are not improved by the dreadful sofa in the waiting room and, when her husband dies, her modest ambition is to raise enough money from the sale of next year's WI calendar to buy the hospital the 'John Clarke Memorial Settee'. With Chris at her side she presents the group with a selection of calendars that have outsold pictures of churches in recent years. In short, the proposal is that, instead of producing a WI calendar of spectacular views, they will produce a calendar of spectacular views of the WI!

We get the photo shoot out of the way at the end of act one, just in time for any outraged members of the audience to storm out. Act two deals with the media frenzy, the fame and the effects that the girls' actions have on the lives of complete strangers who find, to their astonishment, that they are able to smile at a picture on a page that has the word 'leukaemia' on it. The play ends with the revelation of how much money they have raised – the target was five hundred and nineteen pounds – and, though I won't be giving anything away by saying that they raised considerably more than that, it is impossible not to be moved by the warmth, compassion and downright decency of these women.

CALLING TIME
Author: Derek Webb
Publisher: New Theatre Publications
ISBN NO: 9781840948318
Cast: Min 2M 2F
Type: One Act Plays

Calling Time is unusual in that as well as having variable casting it also has a variable running time due to the play being made up of standalone scenes. The author states that so long as the opening and closing scenes, the 'bookends' as he calls them, are performed together with a scene entitled 'Who's Joe' any of the other scenes may be abandoned at the director's will.

The play is set in a local pub and we start with the landlord, Bill, being given a bit of a hard time by the barmaid (or to be politically correct, barperson), Tracy, who is off stage. It seems that Bill has allowed his hand to brush against Tracy and he now finds himself facing allegations of sexual harassment; hence the political correctness. However, their differences are swiftly resolved and we are into the next scene, 'Goodbye Simon', which features a woman whose new hobby is suspiciously coincidental given the manner of her husband's recent death. 'What's Yours' is the story of a blind date where the couple have more in common than either imagined followed by 'Mr Critchley Isn't It?' where a journalist tries to get one over a politician. Thank goodness he didn't try to take out a super-injunction! In 'I Know What You're Thinking' Tim and Rebecca are doing precisely that and then we are into the penultimate scene, 'Who's Joe'. This is quite an intriguing piece which will, indeed, have the audience pondering the title character. Finally in the last scene, Tracy has to clear up the mess the others have left behind.

Calling Time is not the first play to be made up of inter-connected scenes; Alan Ayckbourne's celebrated Confusions is, perhaps, the finest example of the genre, but Derek Webb has produced a play that is worthy of comparison. The greatest dilemma for a director would be which scenes, if any, could be omitted.

CALLING
Author: Colin and Mary Crowther
Publisher: Samuel French
ISBN NO: 9780573033872
Cast: 6F
Type: Full length

Six strangers arrive for a residential weekend during which they will be subjected to tasks, team building exercises and interviews. Sounds a bit like Big Brother but the prize for these young women is the opportunity to answer the calling – to be a nun.

The characters are extremely well defined. Kat is always on the attack due to her low self esteem, but genuinely cares about the people around her. Ann is nervous and dominated by what her father wants for her, but seems to be on the point of rebelling. Caro is very insecure and desperate to have friends, but not willing to make the necessary sacrifices for that to happen. Robyn is an ambitious hard nut but has a soft centre. Patricia is the sensible one whilst Stephanie, who appears aloof at first, is eventually revealed to be very comfortable with herself.

Calling is an uplifting play that demonstrates how strangers can change and grow by being together. The moments of pathos are nicely balanced by some very good comedy, the pace is excellent and the authors have demonstrated a lot of skill in creating characters that an audience will instantly care about.

CANTERBURY TALE, A
Author: Richard Macaulay
Publisher: Drama Association of Wales
ISBN NO: 1898740860
Cast: 7M 3F
Type: One act

A Canterbury Tale is set in the parlour of The Hope Inn, Canterbury, in 1388. Geoffrey Chaucer has been summoned by his friend, Sir Simon Burley, to warn him that they are in danger. A group of Barons are bringing charges of treason against anyone who had been close to the young Richard II. Before leaving the city, Chaucer had been comptroller of the Port of London, whilst Burley was the Constable of Dover Castle and Warden of the Cinque Ports. Although Chaucer does not believe his former position is important enough to justify his arrest, Burley is preparing to flee, but just as he is pulling on his boots, the Kings Marshall arrives and he is arrested.

They had been joined in the parlour by a haphazard assembly of pilgrims and local characters, one of whom, the slimy Stoate, points out Chaucer to the Marshall who concurs that he is, indeed, 'on the list'. However, the others make a fool out of the Marshall and Chaucer is spared.

A Canterbury Tale is an ambitious one act play. The dialogue feels authentic, yet is easy to follow and the story is, at least in part, based on historical fact. The clever thing, though, is that the persons assembled in the inn are the characters that are featured in Chaucer's Canterbury Tales.

CARDENIO
Author: Gregory Doran
Publisher: Nick Hern Books
ISBN NO: 9781848421806
Cast: 12M 5F
Type: Full Length

The Duke of Aguilar hires Cardenio to be a good influence on his son, Fernando, but matters go awry when Fernando develops an obsession for Cardenio's long term lover and a wedding is arranged. Fleeing to the mountains in grief Cardenio meets a farmer's daughter disguised as a boy who tells of her assault at the hands of Fernando then,sickened by his own inability to control his lust Fernando begs forgiveness. This is Cardenio described on the back cover of the script as 'Shakespeare's lost play re-imagined.'

Not included in either of the Bard's portfolios, the authenticity of the original manuscript is something that scholars have argued about for centuries. A play with the title The History of Cardenio by "Mr Fetcher and Shakespeare" is listed in the Stationer's Register of 1653 but it was not published. Fifty years later a copy of the manuscript, not in either of the supposed authors' handwriting, fell into the hands of Lewis Theobald, a writer of pantomimes at Lincoln Fields Inn, who adapted it, and finally published it as Double Falsehood. His version of the play is often mocked but, to be fair, his adaptation suited the audience of the time and it enjoyed a successful run at Drury Lane.

When, in 2003, Gregory Doran sat down with a group of actors to read Double Falsehood he realised, that by comparing the text with the book on which it is based, Miguel de Cervantes' Don Quixote, it should be possible to re-construct the scenes cut by Theobold and produce something close to what the afore-mentioned Mr Fletcher and Shakespeare had written. The resulting play was performed by The Royal Shakespeare Company at Stratford Upon Avon in April 2011.

Though academically interesting, and a success for the RSC, I have reservations about the suitability of the script for amateur companies. There is a temptation to try to spot the bits that have been added to Theobald's manuscript and, whilst the quality is high, it doesn't compare well with Shakespeare at his best.

CARRY ME KATE
Author: Rachel Musgrove
Publisher: Samuel French
ISBN NO: 9780573120367
Cast: 6M 2f
Type: One Act

Dave and Kate: thrown together by a misunderstanding and deciding that, perhaps, it was meant to be. They meet at a Tupperware party; Dave seems to have overlooked the word 'Tupperware' and has turned up with a crate of beer. What Kate sees in him is anybody's guess but they agree to go on a date which is such a disaster that it is a wonder that either of them want to see each other again.

But Kate is besotted with Dave and arranges a mini break for them in the Lake District where she accepts his proposal for marriage; a proposal that Dave didn't realise that he had made.

Carry Me Kate is a cheerful little one act play that carries us along on a combination of live action and direct addresses to the audience. For the most part it is a play that is written to amuse rather than produce belly laughs but it does build to a very entertaining climax and will leave an audience smiling.

CASTRO'S BEARD
Author: Brian Stewart
Publisher: Josef Weinberger
ISBN NO: 9780856763267
Cast: 4M
Type: Full length

It is the eve of Fidel Castro's historic visit to the United Nations Assembly in New York in 1960 and the CIA have hastily assembled a think tank whose aim is to find a way to bring down the Castro regime. As the play starts so does the clandestine meeting, a convenient way to meet the characters and discover their mission. The author wastes no time in mocking the all powerful CIA operatives through their inability to get the overhead projector to function or even find a working flip chart pen – other than a pink one, and what self respecting CIA operative would write with a pink pen so soon after the end of the McCarthy era?

As the four characters come up with increasingly bizarre ideas, one wonders how much of it is true. Did the US government really consider an offer from the Mafia to take care of Castro in return for turning a blind eye to a few wrong doings? Did the CIA seriously discuss sending the Cuban dictator gifts such as socks that make a beard fall out, or exploding cigars. Well, looking at the bibliography at the back of the script, it seems that they did.

Stewart's script is clearly very well researched and the characters, though a little two dimensional at times, convey the hysteria that we associate with the United States and Communism during this period of their history. The play starts at quite a frenetic pace and slows down as we go on. Although divided into two acts, it might be worth considering the author's suggestion to play it all the way through as act two might come as something of an anticlimax otherwise.

A play about a CIA plot to bring down Fidel Castro might not be an obvious choice for a society in rural England but there is plenty of humour, and poking fun at powerful organisations is always enjoyable.

CCTV
Author: Derek Webb
Publisher: New Theatre Publications
ISBN NO: 9781840947649
Cast: 3M 1F
Type: One Act

We are in the security control room of The Oaks, a large shopping centre. The forth wall is covered in CCTV monitors which means that this is one of those very rare plays where it is absolutely natural for the actors to face the audience throughout the action.

The play opens with the arrival of Rick, here to start the night shift, taking over duties from Alex and Jane, the latter having just nipped out for a bit of last minute shopping. The banter between the two men is most entertaining and the author skilfully uses this to establish the scenario for the audience.

The dull routine of life in a security office is blown away with the arrival of Keith, who has a stocking over his head and a gun in the back of the apologetic Jane. The horror of the situation is somewhat diluted by the fact that neither Rick nor Alex can make out a single word that Keith is saying, due to the afore mentioned stocking. The humour comes thick and fast. Alex unwittingly tells Keith all he needs to know, whilst Rick insists that people adhere to the correct use of grammar, whatever the circumstances. CCTV is a well written, very funny one act play that is sure to please.

CELEBULITE
Author: Derek Webb
Publisher: New Theatre Publications
ISBN NO: 9781840946826
Cast: 1M 3F
Type: One Act

Celebulite is a one act play about the cult of celebrity. Victoria is a minor sleb who wakes up one morning to find herself looking 20 years older: a middle aged woman staring back at her from the mirror when she is only in her mid twenties. Russell has suffered a similar fate: he has suddenly gained 5 stones. It is an intriguing premise but I feel that this play fails to explore its potential. We start off with an unnecessarily long conversation between Victoria and Katherine, a cleaner, who is described as 'working class and proud of it' but whose language doesn't really seem to fit this description. Things don't really seem to be heading anywhere until Russell appears and we get the reveal about the changes in appearance. There are some pretty heavy hints that perhaps these people are older/fatter than they liked to think they were, so when the end comes there are no real surprises.

I think more could have been made of this idea. The characters are a bit two dimensional, which may be a deliberate attempt to make them look like Reality TV personalities. However this makes it difficult to like them or to care about what happens to them, and there isn't enough humour for a play which is supposed to be witty. The cult of celebrity is certainly a hot topic at the moment but it is a shame that this play doesn't quite live up to its promise.

CHESHIRE CATS
Author: Gail Young
Publisher: Samuel French
ISBN NO: 978057311081
Cast: 1M 5F with Doubling
Type: Full Length

A tale of aching feet and heaving bosoms! Meet the Cheshire Cats; a team of fund raisers planning to walk thirteen miles across London in a record time in their posh trainers and decorative bras.

With its roots in amateur theatre, Cheshire Cats was first performed by Guilden Sutton Players in their village hall in 2005. The play became a hit at Edinburgh Fringe Festival and is now published by Samuel French. quite an achievement for its author.

We begin with Maggie and Vicky exercising as they wait for the others to join them. Vicky is the fit one for whom the stretching and bending comes naturally whilst Maggie, on the other hand, is out of shape in more ways than one. It is a rather clumsy start as the pair set the scene accompanied by comedy bordering on slapstick, but then the others arrive and we meet Andrew, a Hugh Grant type charmer that Vicky has recently met. When we learn that one of the women has failed to turn up for yet another training session I think we can guess where we are heading.

Chester Railway Station is the first destination and the women assemble to catch the train to London. As expected, Vicky arrives with Andrew and advises that he is to be the replacement for her sister, the one that has been missing the training sessions. Once on the train Andrew comes over as more Sid James than Hugh Grant and there is resentment that he is spoiling their girls' weekend, but they put on a brave face, start a game of Jenga and chug off to the interval.

After the break we are in London for the walk. The women, and Andrew, are in their pink Cheshire Cat outfits and set off, soon becoming separated due to their varied abilities. This is where we learn the reason for Andrew's out-of-character behaviour on the train and get a hint of the reason why he wanted to take part in the walk: it isn't just to be with Vicky, as we find out at the very end.

It is inevitable that comparisons will be drawn between this play and Calendar Girls. Both feature a group of women performing in an event to raise money for a cancer charity, of course, but another thing they have in common is that, despite Cheshire Cats being partially in verse, there is a reliance on the visual elements of the script rather than any subtlety in the text. But I don't want to be too harsh. I have no doubt that it will have lots of successful productions in the amateur world where it started its life.

CHRISTMAS CAROL, A
Author: Adapted by Stephen Sharkey
Publisher: Josef Weinberger
ISBN NO: 9780856763212
Cast: 6M 4F plus chorus.
Type: Full length

My first thought on picking up this script was, 'Does the world really need another adaptation of A Christmas Carol?' but as Stephen Sharkey has an impressive track record of adapting classics for the modern stage, I had high hopes that this reworking of the Dickens' tale would be worth reading.

I am pleased to say that my time was not wasted. The author has taken a fresh look at the story and focussed on what made Scrooge the man that he was, thereby adding depth that is usually missing from modern interpretations. A Christmas Carol is a dark tale and Sharkey has remained faithful to the original, which means that this version is probably not suitable for a very young audience. However children over seven, and adults, will enjoy the contrast of the doom and gloom of Scrooge's existence compared to the simple pleasures enjoyed by the Cratchit family.

A quick search on an on line bookseller revealed over two hundred versions of A Christmas Carol in the drama section alone, but if your theatre company is considering putting it on then I would highly recommend this adaptation.

CLICK OF THE HEELS, A
Author: Eleanor Fossey
Publisher: J Garnett Miller
ISBN NO: 9780853436638
Cast: 1F
Type: Monologue

Pauline, middle-aged and overweight, stands before us in her swimming costume, a towel wrapped around her to hide what she sees as her unsightly flesh. She starts to chat. In her conversational manner she tells us about her experiences of bikini waxing, why she calls fast swimmers 'juliennes' and of how she auditioned for the part of Dorothy in The Wizard of Oz when she was a girl.

Despite clicking her heels until her ankles were sore she didn't get the part and was instead asked to be Chief Munchkin. She was ideal for the role, explained her teacher, because she was 'responsible'. Pauline explains to us that, in the language of school auditions, 'responsible' means 'fat'.

This disappointment paved the way for the attitude that Pauline was to have to life. Instead of following the yellow brick road the path she chose was a comfortable beige. Amongst all this self effacing humour there is pathos as well as some real laugh out loud moments such as her description of men's hairstyles: parted, unparted and departed.

Then Pauline meets Max and her life changes forever, though not in a way that we might have expected. She embarks on a new venture during which she learns that it was not the magic slippers that gave Dorothy the power to shape her life but the things that she had all along: courage, enthusiasm and love.

This is a very well written monologue which will give an actress the opportunity to run the gauntlet of emotions before we reach the uplifting conclusion.

CLING TO ME LIKE IVY
Author: Samantha Ellis
Publisher: Nick Hern Books
ISBN NO: 9781848420656
Cast: 3M 3F
Type: Full length

Cling To Me Like Ivy was inspired by Sheitel-gate; an event that, I admit, passed me by but that had huge impact in the orthodox Jewish world. Incredibly, the whole thing was sparked by a chance remark from Victoria Beckham when, during a TV interview, she was asked if the hair in her extensions came from Russian prisons. She made light of it but it sparked an investigation into the origin of the hair that makes up the wigs, or sheitels, worn by married orthodox Jewish women who cover their heads according to rules of modesty. It was a Rabbi who discovered that much of the hair came from a Hindu temple in India where the hair was removed from women's heads as part of a religious ceremony. As Hindus worship Idols it was suggested that the wearing of these wigs contravened Jewish law.

Samantha Ellis' play centres around Rivka, a young Jewish woman who has just bought her first sheitel ahead of her impending wedding; her relationship with her father, a Rabbi, and her best friend Leela who is Hindu. Rivka's grandmother, fiancé and Leela's tree-saving boyfriend, Patrick, make up the rest of the characters, all of whom play an important role as the story develops. The play is beautifully written: the dialogue has pace and humour, the characters are engaging and the storyline is sharp and elegant.

The turmoil caused by Sheitel-gate leads to Rivka questioning her faith until, full of doubt, she crosses a line. Then, having taken that small step, she rushes headlong into a world that she barely knew existed. She joins Patrick in his tree protest. The pair drink kosher wine followed by beer and Bourbon Creams before making love. In the morning she is arrested and then brought home by her father to answer for her behaviour. She has no answers, only questions, but in an emotional climax a father's love for his daughter defeats all other concerns.

Cling To Me Like Ivy is an intelligent play. It educates and informs yet is accessible, witty and always entertaining: A remarkable piece of theatre from a supremely talented playwright.

CLYBOURNE PARK

Author: Bruce Norris
Publisher: Nick Hern Books
ISBN NO: 9781842421325
Cast: 5M 3F
Type: Full length

It is 1959 and we are in Clybourne Park, a cosy suburb of Chicago. Russ and Bev have sold their desirable two-bed property for a knock down price, bringing it to within the reach of the type of people who would not normally be able to afford a house in Clybourne Park. The suburb is about to get its first black family.

As the play begins, Russ and Bev come over as quite a charming couple. Their amusing conversation about how Neapolitan ice cream got its name is typical of nineteen-fifties innocence. The cheery atmosphere is maintained following the arrival of Jim, though the author cleverly brings depth to the characters by allowing the dialogue to occasional stray from the mundane.

The black characters, Francine and Alfred, who are not the purchasers of the property, at first seem peripheral to the action. Perhaps this is an allusion to the attitude of the time. Francine is Bev's 'helper' and they get along fine. The neighbours also like her, but the idea of a black family actually owning a property in the street seems unimaginable. Where would they worship? Where would they shop for their 'ethnic' food items? Francine's husband, Alfred, teases by saying that he would never shop anywhere that didn't sell pigs' feet. Things are gradually turning more serious when one of the neighbours suggests that the sale could be halted, reasoning that a black family in the street would start an exodus of white people away from the area. Tension mounts and, when the reason why Russ and Bev are selling their house for a knock down price is revealed, the neighbours are shocked. We end act one with an exchange between Bev and Albert that epitomises the unintentionally condescending attitude that some good natured white people had toward black acquaintances at the time.

Act two and it is 2009. The house has been modernised, but on-the-cheap, and is a scruffy shadow of its former self. Lindsay and Steve are buying the property and plan to knock it down and start again.
We have an inconsequential conversation that is reminiscent of the one between Russ and Bev in the first act and the fact that the same

actors are now playing different roles, and that their characters have links to the past, helps with the continuity. The issue of racism comes up again, reminding us of how little has changed over the last fifty years. Just as before, the white folk do not consider themselves to be racist but their words prove otherwise. This time the response from the black characters is much more explicit and in a powerful and disturbing scene the characters attempt to out-do each other by telling offensive 'jokes'. The stage direction "all hell breaks loose" about sums it up until the play ends by completing the link with the past with the appearance of a previously unseen character from act one.

Clybourne Park is satirical, shocking, funny and provocative: a powerful, challenging and exciting piece of drama that is most definitely this month's play of the month.

CODPIECES
Author: Perry Pontac
Publisher: Oberon Books
ISBN NO: 978184949430555
Cast: Various
Type: Three Act

Codpieces comprises three Shakespearean parodies that first saw the light of day on BBC radio.

In the first, Hamlet II, Perry Pontac attempts to answer the question "What happened next?"

The opening dialogue reminds me of the very first episode of the TV series Red Dwarf when Dave Lister wakes from a long sleep and asks the computer what has happened to his companions. As he names each of them the response is always the same: "Dead, Dave", and in Hamlet II Seltazer is getting a similar, if more poetic, response from Fornia. Every good scholar knows that at the end of Hamlet everyone dies, and now Seltazar knows it too. But the situation is not beyond hope. Fornia has studied long and hard and found an honourable and rightful successor to claim the crown of Denmark: none other than the noble Macbeth. Alas, Seltazer has just arrived from Scotia and it is now his turn to impart bad news. With no one to reign, the fate of Denmark would appear to rest with this pair until an unlikely stranger appears. There is no happy ending though. At the end of Hamlet II everyone dies.

In the second parody it is a question of "What happened first?" as we enter the palace of Prince Lear who receives a surprising piece of information from the Earl of Kent. The intention of this playlet is to create the scene that opens King Lear and so, despite the extraordinary tale, it all seems to make sense in the end.

The final parody is Fatal Loins which ask another question in its own prologue: "If Juliet and Romeo survive will their eternal passion stay alive?" Er, no. The once star-crossed lovers are now in the middle age of their discontent. Juliet is as vast as a cathedral and Romeo loves another: Friar Lawrence. The holy man's attempt to right what has gone wrong backfires and, though the pair had survived for twenty more years, Romeo and Juliet eventually succumb to the fate that Shakespeare described.

Codpieces is witty, intelligent and beautifully written. It truly is the language of Shakespeare, with the occasional truly awful joke, and keeps alive the art of the brilliant parody.

COMMON DENOMINATOR
Author: Sue Welch
Publisher: J Garnett Miller
ISBN NO: 9780853436782
Cast: 2M 15F
Type: One Act

We are in the ladies loos of a nightclub on a Saturday night. The fourth wall is lined with sinks with mirrors above so it is natural that the steady flow of ladies wishing to spend a penny face the audience as they fix their make-up. The first group to powder their noses are teenagers including a girl called Annie whom I immediately took to due to her use of the phrase 'hunky dory'. I don't think I have ever heard anyone use it in real life but it is such eccentric phrase I am all for its promotion.

Common Denominator is essentially the story of relationships: cheating boyfriends, desperate women and tiresome mothers. As we witness these little slices of life – in one case, new life – we are challenged to consider the common denominator. What is it that links the stories of these women? The answer is the way that they find to cope with the things that are happening around them, choosing what works best for the individual, whether that is facing problems head on or sweeping them under the carpet. With moments of comedy and of high drama Common Denominator is another excellent festival candidate from Sue Welch.

CONVERSATIONS IN HALLWAYS
Author: Carole Bugge
Publisher: www.productionscripts.com
ISBN NO: none
Cast: 3M 3F 1M Voice
Type: Full length

Conversations in Hallways is a warm and funny play about relationships. Harry and Carl are best friends: Harry is seeing Michelle but things are not well between them; and the three of them are all currently rehearsing a musical that has great music, but dreadful lyrics written by the ultra-confident Steve. Michelle flirts with Carl but Harry seems unconcerned. He considers 'Jealousy (to be) an outmoded expression'. Exasperated, Michelle asks Carl, in front of Harry and Steve, if he would like to sleep with her. He would, of course, and Harry refuses to stand in his way. Carl almost begs him to tell him to 'keep my hands off your girl'. But, to Harry, it is politically incorrect to consider another person as a possession.

Just as we become convinced that Harry is an insensitive fool the story takes a turn and we realise that his behaviour is an attempt to help Michelle overcome her deep seated insecurity. Then we learn that Michelle is not quite what she seems, nor indeed is she how Harry describes her. As the characters reveal hidden depths they become more real and this makes the somewhat surprising twists in the tale more acceptable. I enjoyed this play: it is uplifting, engaging and written with great skill.

CRANFORD
Author: Elizabeth Gaskell adapted by Campbell Kay
Publisher: The Phoenix Press
ISBN NO: 9780956630803
Cast: 6M 16F or 2M 8F with doubling
Type: Full length

Cranford was originally published in serial form in Household Words when Elizabeth Gaskell was approached by Charles Dickens to make a contribution to the periodical. It was published as a novel in 1853 and, after the author's death three years later, its popularity has meant it has never been out of print, the recent BBC production bringing the story to a whole new audience. Campbell Kay's adaptation was first produced by Nottingham Arts Theatre in 2009.

In a society dominated by an older generation of somewhat snobbish women the philosophy of living to a moral code, with an emphasis on humanity and kindness, is put to the test with the onset of the industrial revolution, rising crime and economic crisis.

As our story begins the ladies of Cranford neatly set the scene and we are immersed into their rather quaint world where anything at odds with the moral code is considered 'vulgar'. But we are immediately made aware that things are changing: the arrival of the railway into the town has offended their sensibilities. As Miss Pole points out, "If God has meant us to travel by steam locomotive he would have given us furnaces instead of bellies and stove pipes instead of heads."

There is a good deal of humour in the script but the underlying theme is that of change. The ladies are struggling to come to terms with the way society is evolving and there are many priceless moments, for example Miss Pole's gentle remark when complimenting a friend on her connections "Of course, I am not related to anyone in trade myself". To condense the whole of Cranford into a couple of hour's entertainment is quite an achievement but Campbell Kay has pulled it off by concentrating on the essential elements of the story. As a result, whilst the script has pace, it does not feel rushed or incomplete.

It is well known that Cranford is modelled on Knutsford in Cheshire and my own associations with that town sparked in me a natural interest in this new adaptation but, with a script as well crafted as this one, Campbell Kay's play should have universal appeal.

CRASH
Author: Andrew Fusek Peters & Polly Peters
Publisher: dbda
ISBN NO: 9781902843308
Cast: Min 2M 2F

Have you ever wondered what story lies behind a bunch of flowers left at the side of the road? Perhaps they have been tied to a tree damaged by being struck by a vehicle. Crash is a story told in verse that imagines the tragedy that lies behind this sad token of loss and how it affects those left behind.

Having played their first gig the teenage members of rock band Stormboy are on a roll. For Nat, the lead singer, life is great and when he starts to go out with Kate, a girl from that first gig, his head is buzzing; he cannot rest. In the verse of the text he is obsessed. Their romance continues through the summer and we might sympathise with their frustration of learning to be intimate whilst struggling to obtain privacy.

One of the band members, Carl, has an advantage over his young friends: he drives a car. It is he at the wheel on the fateful night as they drive back from a rehearsal. The blinding evening sun becomes headlights and Nat loses his life when the car leaves the road. We know this is coming but the authors still manage to stir our emotions when Kate, on learning the news, can manage only one word: no.

Original and literate, Crash will appeal to a teenage audience and the quality of the writing is of such a standard that it works well as a piece to be dissected and discussed in addition to being an affecting piece of theatre.

DANCING TO THE SOUND OF CRUNCHING SNAILS
Author: Joe Graham
Publisher: J Garnet Miller
ISBN NO: 9780853436621
Cast: 2M 2F

Katie, a woman in her early twenties, is busying herself in the kitchen, nervously humming along to The Blue Danube as it plays on the stereo. She is obviously trying to mentally prepare herself for an ordeal ahead. Meanwhile, Sam, her husband is in the living room completely immersed in honing his skill in the fine and ancient art of, er, Buckaroo. Finding the Strauss waltz distracting he swaps the music for the genius that is Mike Batt and the air is filled with the sound of A Wombling Merry Christmas.

Joe Graham has shown good skill here. Within the first minute he has introduced us to some characters that it is hard not to like, established that it is Christmas and that, for Katie at least, there is tension in the air. We might guess that, due to the season, the cause of that tension is families.

Before long Katie's sister arrives, but she is not the cause of this tension. Through little clues in the dialogue we realise that the sisters' father is what is causing Katie to be so anxious. She has not seen him since she was a small girl and her parents divorced. The nervousness at meeting her father is tinged with resentment.;a feeling that he abandoned them at a time when they didn't understand what was happening. Katie's memories of her father are so remote she does not know what is real and what was planted into her head by her mother so that, when the meeting comes, you could cut the air with a knife. Perhaps it is he knife that Katie was, until recently, threatening to use for self harm as a way of avoiding the meeting all together.

Fortunately for all concerned, Father turns out to be good natured, jolly and, by his own admission, a big fan of Buckaroo. All families have secrets though and we haven't quite reached the "all live happily ever" after stage just yet.

The author does very well to avoid any clichés with the storyline and, as the significance of the play's title and of The Blue Danube is revealed, we have a sense of having been on a journey with the characters. This is quite an achievement and I found Dancing to the Sound of Crunching Snails to be a very satisfying piece of theatre.

DAVID COPPERFIELD

Author: Charles Dickens adapted by Alastair Cording
Publisher: Nick Hern Books
ISBN NO: 9781848420229
Cast: 13M 11F
Type: Full length

Alastair Cording's adaptation whisks us through the Dickens's classic at a cracking pace as the story is told over forty six scenes. The speed of the action means that there is a danger that audiences may miss some of the more subtle elements, but those familiar with the tale will be pleased to note that Barkis is willing and the eccentric Mr McAwber is most confident that something will turn up.

The humour comes over well, as does the cruelty inflicted on David and others by Uriah Heep, Murdstone, Steerforth and Mr Creakle. Audiences should enjoy this tale of relationships and how the behaviour of adults has such a profound influence on the children around them.

DEAD HEAVY FANTASTIC

Author: Robert Farquhar
Publisher: Josef Weinberger
ISBN NO: 9780856763182
Cast: 4M 4F
Type: Full length

Sex and drugs and karaoke: Liverpool on a Friday night and Frank is sitting in a trendy bar waiting for his blind date. He doesn't have to wait very long. Cindy arrives, introduces herself, asks for a drink (double vodka – straight) and tells Frank that he has a nice face. She reminds him of her Dad. No, not now. When he was younger, in his forties. Frank tells her that he is thirty-nine. Cindy apologies and gets up to leave; but she doesn't go. Instead she suggests they go somewhere together. She knows a place that isn't far. She has some condoms…

Dead Heavy Fantastic is a whirlwind of a play, the speed of Cindy's proposition a metaphor for the pace of the action. Keep up. You won't want to miss anything!

As you would expect from a play set in the streets, bars and nightclubs of Liverpool, not to mention the Accident and Emergency department of the local hospital, the language is colourful and our story encompasses all the unsavoury aspects of a drunken night out that goes horribly wrong. It is also very, very funny. Characters enter and leave the action to provide momentary glimpses into the lives of people who are not in control of their own destiny. They supply humour and pathos in equal measure in this slice of Friday night that is both fascinating and frightening.

In the hotel where Cindy takes Frank we meet Vince, Cindy's desperate ex-boyfriend who is prepared to do anything to get her back. Frank's evening gets increasingly weird as he is drawn into Vince's world of girls, drugs, booze and a little bit of arson on the side. Frank is out of his depth in so many ways but in spite of himself he ends up the hero. Most of the characters in this play are the type that we would cross the road to avoid but one cannot help hoping that everything is going to work out ok for all of them and I was relieved that, for Frank at least, there is a happy ending.

Any company considering putting on a production of Dead Heavy Fantastic would have to use every warning they have available but, for the broad minded, this is a fantastically good play.

DISCO PIGS
Author: Enda Walsh
Publisher: Nick Hern Books in the Compilation "Plays One"
ISBN NO: 9781848421394
Cast: 1M 1F
Type: Full length

Disco Pigs is the play that brought Enda Walsh to attention when it opened in Cork and Dublin in 1996 followed by runs in Edinburgh and London. It tells the story of Pig and Runt; two teenagers who have a relationship so close that it is almost telepathic. As they grow up they are barely aware of the outside world but, when Runt receives attention from another boy, Pig becomes violent.

Written for Eileen Walsh, who played Runt in the original production, Disco Pigs is a messed up jumble of extraordinary language and explosive action. With much to liken it to Irvine Walsh's Trainspotting, this is something that is likely to divide opinion but, love it or hate it, there is no denying the inventiveness of the creator.

DISCONNECT
Author: Anupama Chandrasekhar
Publisher: Nick Hern Books
ISBN NO: 9781848420854
Cast: 3M 2F
Type: Full length

A couple of years ago the newspapers were full of stories about call centres based in India where the staff were taught to speak with English accents and watched episodes of Eastenders and Coronation Street in an attempt to fool customers into believing that they were based in the UK. These stories encouraged us to be either amused or scandalised (depending on the newspaper) that the operators knew precisely what the weather was currently like in our part of the country but had no idea whether Newcastle was north or south of London. Then, as more British companies started to 'offshore' their call centres, and people started to lose jobs, there was a noticeable backlash against this practice. A friend of mine, who worked on a help desk, was once challenged by a caller as to where, precisely, the help desk was located. The answer to that question was 'Crewe' and my friend is, in fact, Welsh.

Disconnect is based at a call centre in Chennai, India, where the operators are chasing payments owed to an American credit card company. Avinash is one of the supervisors and is being given a dressing down by his young boss Jyothi. The problem is that he is under-performing and cannot be allowed to remain in his section that is responsible for collecting payments from customers in New York. He is, effectively, being demoted and moved to Illinois – a small team on the fourth floor.

Life in Illinois is frenetic. Ross, Vidya and Giri are constantly on the telephone trying to persuade their 'delinquent' customers to make payments on their cards whilst there is much chat amongst themselves between and even during calls. Avinash doesn't like what he sees. He believes in doing things by the book and this team, Ross in particular, breaks all the rules.

For the workers in the call centre one day is pretty much like the next. It's the same old thing day after day and, unfortunately, I felt that the same could be said for the many scenes in this play. As the plot develops, Ross foolishly falls for one of his customers and commits a serious breach of policy; Vidya is devastated to learn that one of her customers took his own life soon after her call demanding payment and Giri eventually escapes life in the call centre, but there was too little variety to keep me interested.

DRIVING FORCE
Author: Sue Welch
Publisher: J Garnett Miller
ISBN NO: 4780853436768
Cast: 3M 3F or 2M 4F
Type: One Act

Driving Force is a tale of guilt and lies. Alan's life is a mess: his marriage is on the rocks, he drinks too much and he is at risk of losing his job. When he knocks down a girl whilst driving too fast he doesn't stop; if he reports the accident his wife will want to know what he is doing in that part of town when his work place is in a different direction and his infidelity will be revealed. He doesn't know if the girl is dead or alive, hence the guilt. The lies started years ago.

Laura is in a coma, her parents at her bedside. The doctor says that he thinks she will be all right but it is hard to tell until she wakes up. Meanwhile, Alan is having hallucinations. He imagines that he is being visited by Laura, thinking that she is a ghost but when the story of the hit and run appears in a paper it says that the victim is in a coma. Somehow that is worse.

This is the type of play where we expect a twist and many people will, like me, think they have worked out what it is going to be, but Sue Welch is smarter than that. Yes, we get the expected twist but then there is another one, just to make it that bit more interesting.

The characterisation is excellent. Alan and his wife can barely stand each other but they loved each once and the author hasn't forgotten that. Laura's parents have a much more stable relationship but, at times like these when the cracks begin to show, this is subtly done. Driving Force is an opportunity for actors to show us what they can do and I am particularly pleased to see a strong role for a teenager in an adult play.

DUETS
Author: Peter Quilter
Publisher: Samuel French
ISBN NO: 9780573111112
Cast: Min 1M 1F
Type: Full Length

Duets is a collection of four short plays that may be performed individually or as a single production. Each play examines relationships and features just two characters, hence the title and the suggested link music to bridge the scenes.

The first of the plays is 'Blind Date' which introduces us to an elderly pair seeking romance. Although the bespectacled Wendy and the toupee'd Jonathan were both clearly economical with the truth when they described themselves in a dating magazine, when Wendy arrives at Jonathan's apartment, clutching a huge block of cheese, she does not seem too disappointed. Quilter beautifully captures the nervousness of two strangers trying to make light-hearted conversation, and the scene works very well if one is able to put aside the idea that it is unlikely that any woman would agree to meet a stranger at his apartment.

The second story concerns Barrie, a successful gay man who cannot live without the organisational skills of secretary, Janet, who is looking for a husband. The trouble is that she doesn't want any old husband, she wants Barrie and, despite the obvious impediment, the arrangement does seem to have its advantages.

In 'Holiday', Bobby and Shelly have decided to go to Spain and consume a large number of cocktails before discussing the finer points of their forthcoming divorce and, in the final story, Angela is about to embark on her third marriage regardless of the fact that all the signs are that this is a very bad idea.

In all four plays the characters are believable and endearing whilst the dialogue is entertaining throughout. My one reservation is that, at times, the script reads like a series of gags. For example, Wendy's vegetarian ex-husband and Barrie's order for a new bed have no relevance to the plot and were forgotten after a couple of funny lines which would have been more at home in a stand up comedy routine than a piece of theatre.

EDGAR AND ANNABEL
Author: Sam Holcroft
Publisher: Nick Hern Books
ISBN NO: 9781848422193
Cast: 4M 3F
Type: Long One Act

Edgar and Annabel is published within Double Feature, the first of two volumes published by Nick Hern Books which bring together four authors who have received their first commissions from the National Theatre. A review of the second play in this volume, The Swan, is included in this month's column.

Sam Holcroft has written some of the most interesting plays that I have read in the last couple of years. Reviews of While You Sleep and Pink have appeared in these pages and her inventive and prolific output bodes well for the future of British theatre.

Edgar and Annabel starts with familiar domesticity. Marianne is in the kitchen preparing a salad and when Nick comes in his first line, 'Hi, honey, I'm home.' emphasises the ordinariness of it all. Why then does Marianne turn round and stare at Nick in disbelief for a few moments before going on with her routine? When Nick then produces two scripts from his briefcase, and the scene continues with the pair reading their lines, it is clear that something very much out of the ordinary is occurring in this domestic setting. We begin to understand what is going on when, under the cover of the sound made by an electric carving knife, Nick gets Marianne to hide some documents. Echoes here of Big Brother is watching you; or, in this case, listening.

Nick and Marianne are playing the roles of Edgar and Annabel as their contribution to a resistance movement seeking to overthrow a totalitarian government. They are attempting to give the illusion of normality whilst their house is, in fact, a bomb factory. Nick is actually a replacement for an operative who has been arrested. He is the new Edgar, provided by the movement so that the authorities don't link the man they have arrested with the property that houses three gallons of petrochemicals. This explains Marianne's surprise and, in a meeting with their coordinator, she expresses her anger.

There is much humour drawn from Nick's initial ineptness at playing the role of Edgar and there is even something for fans of Farndale type comedies as the pair refer to what is clearly a chicken as 'the salmon'. Over time Nick and Marianne begin to grow quite fond of each other, in contrast to their scripts which has them growing apart. The couple host a party and, as the guests take it in turn to sing karaoke, the others set about assembling the bombs. We sense tension as they approach their big day and Nick, unable to take the pressure, finds himself seriously going off the script. The next day, Marianne is again in the kitchen preparing dinner when her husband comes home. But it isn't Nick. There has been another replacement.

Edgar and Annabel is the sort of play that has us pondering long after the final curtain has fallen; not because anything has been left unexplained but because of all the possibilities that the script has created. Were Nick and his predecessor really arrested by the authorities or were they removed by their own organisations? Which is the greater evil: the totalitarian government or its opposition? The fact that an apparently simple tale can have such depth is a sign of a very good writer. Sam Holcroft is innovative and thought provoking but she never forgets that people go to the theatre to be entertained. This is her best yet.

THE EMPEROR'S NEW CLOTHES OR FIVE BEANS FOR JACK
Author: David Foxton
Publisher: Samuel French
ISBN NO: 9780573150111
Cast: 5M 5F plus extras
Type: Children's Full Length

Tom "Tink" Bell, the Town Crier, summons our attention and with great authority and solemnity reads out an important proclamation: "One small brown loaf, half a dozen medium sized eggs..." Oh no! That's his shopping list. OK, it's not the most original joke in the world but it is sure to get the children laughing right from the off. This is important because it sends out a clear signal to a young audience about the type of show they are watching. Writers of pantomimes make great use of this device that can be summarised as follows: there is a joke coming, here it is, the good natured audience laugh at a joke they have heard many times before, and off we go.

Once Tink does eventually find the proclamation he makes such a hash of reading it that he announces that the emperor's birthday is to be celebrated this and every Friday, the costs of which will lead the town into bankruptcy. Meanwhile, a character by the name of Jack has been tricked into selling his cow for a handful of beans by a suspicious pair called Sly and Wily who are also going around the town distributing forged money.

The tricksters ingratiate themselves with the emperor getting him to buy ever more elaborate clothes for his weekly birthday celebrations. They arrange a fashion show but they have two problems. Firstly, they are running out of clothes to sell him and secondly he is running out of money to pay.

The issue of funds is apparently solved by Jack who has found an unexpected source of gold at the top of a beanstalk. This means the emperor can put off raising taxes to pay for a fabulous new outfit Sly and Wily have created for him: an outfit that is completely invisible to anyone who isn't "intelligent, clever, trustworthy and in the right job!" Sadly, not even the discovery of a golden egg laying goose is enough to pay for the huge rise in taxes, so Jack shins up his beanstalk once more and finds a magic harp. Was that "Fee-Fi-Fo-Fum" that I just heard? Meanwhile, the big day has appeared for the emperor to appear in his birthday suit. Well, almost. This is a family show.

There is, of course, a happy ending and it all comes together quite nicely. Anyone looking for something a bit different to a traditional pantomime, but with the same easy sense of fun, would do well to consider this script from David Foxton.

ESSENCE OF LOVE, THE
Author: Philip Ayckbourn
Publisher: Stagescripts
ISBN NO: None
Cast: 2M 2F with doubling
Type: Full Length

Imagine that you are the son of the UK's most popular living playwright and you decide to have a go at writing yourself. What would you do? Write under an assumed name so that nobody can accuse you of using your father's name to give you a leg up in the industry? Or do use your real name and hope people will judge you on your own merit? Philip Ayckbourn has chosen the latter path and must, therefore, accept the inevitable comparisons with Sir Alan.

The Essence of Love is, of course, a love story. On adjoining roof terraces in Marrakesh are Martin with his son, Tom, on one and Diana with her daughter, Gemma, on the other Things are a bit strained for Martin. His son hasn't forgiven him for running off with "that tart" and the only reason Tom is there on the holiday is because his father's latest conquest dumped him after it had been booked and paid for.

Meanwhile, the couple next door seem like an ideal match and we feel romance must be in the air, but the first time Tom speaks to Gemma his attitude is bordering on being rude. However, his behaviour changes dramatically after drinking a magic potion that Diana slips into his water bottle. She got it from a Moroccan street vendor with the promise that the drinker will fall in love with the first person he sees. Unfortunately, having drunk the potion it is Diana that Tom sees rather than Gemma.

With the mismatched pair out on the town, Martin and Gemma are left to try to work out what is going on. Then Gemma chokes on a peanut and Martin passes her Tom's water bottle to take a drink and, of course, Gemma instantly falls in love with Martin.

In an effort to sort it all out Diana purchases an antidote from the street vendor. The potion was free – the antidote is one thousand dirhams – but, with the potion and the antidote in identical phials, this just leads to more confusion, especially when Martin drinks some of the potion then looks in the mirror!

So how does The Essence of Love compare with the plays of Alan Ayckbourn? Well, the elder is no stranger to introducing a fantastical element to an otherwise mundane setting, so the idea of a magic potion in a play aimed at adults has a nice Ayckbourn feel to it. The clear characterisation and the exploration of the nuances of speech make this an accomplished first play but, most importantly, Philip Ayckbourn has found his own voice and produced a script should make his father proud.

EVERYONE
Author: Jo Clifford
Publisher: Nick Hern Books
ISBN NO: 9781848420915
Cast: 3M 3F 1Child plus Dancers
Type: Full length

From the outset we know we are in for something different with Everyone. Once the actors have gone though the preliminaries: 'you first', 'why me?', 'it's your play', much of the dialogue is direct to the audience and we are reminded on more than one occasion that we are watching a play rather than eavesdropping on real people. There is even a description of the theatre in which the play is being performed, something that the author has helpfully offered to adapt to your own particular circumstances should you choose to perform the play. I have read many scripts that have the actors address the audience and they often feel artificial and too artistic for their own good. Everyone does not come into that category: the characters are likeable and it feels as though they speaking to a friend.

Having got to know a little about Mary, her husband, children and mother, the story begins. While the husband, Joe, is shopping and complaining about only being able to get Anya potatoes that are small and knobbly and taste like soap, Mary is home, doing the ironing, when she suffers a brain haemorrhage. Death calls, literally, and what an irritating person he is! Jo Clifford is not afraid to exploit the humour but the story is predominantly moving as the characters come to terms with what has happened, grieving not for the pain that they currently feel, but for the good times of the past that will never be relived.

Everyone is an impressive piece of theatre from an innovative writer.

EX FACTOR, THE

Author: Ian Hornby
Publisher: New Theatre Publications
ISBN NO: 9781840947052
Cast: 3M 4F
Type: Full length

Ian Hornby has been writing am dram friendly comedies and thrillers for more than twenty years and through New Theatre Publications, an organisation he helped found, his extensive catalogue is available for perusal. The Ex Factor is a recent and worthwhile addition to this prolific writer's portfolio.

Phil and his wife, Jane, run a smallholding but are hoping to use their farm house as a Bed and Breakfast establishment. As the play begins they are mid argument, the subject being Fliss, Phil's ex-wife. It seems that she and her new partner are coming to stay and this is not something that fills Jane with joy. In factshe blames Fliss for the fact that they are in such dire straits: so short of cash that she is worried that they are not able to furnish the place to a standard required to obtain a Bed and Breakfast certificate. Then Phil drops a bombshell. The inspector who will be doing the assessment is: his ex-wife, Fliss!

Fliss and her partner arrive, as do Margaret and Anne who had not been expected until the following day. Add in a rustic farmhand and some rather strong potato wine and we are on our farcical way.

The Ex Factor is the sort of play where the audience works out what is going on long before the characters on the stage and the fun is waiting for the penny to drop. The chasing around the room and running in and out of doors is written with confidence and the plot has plenty of twists to keep an audience happy. It can be a challenge to entice the public away from their televisions to watch live theatre but, with writers like Ian Hornby supplying our market, it is good to know that Britain's got talent.

FALLEN ANGELS
Author: Sue Welch
Publisher: J Garnett Miller
ISBN NO: 9780853436713
Cast: 1M 5F
Type: One Act

Five Angels have been sent to a Celestial Punishment Centre due to their misbehaviour. There is Gloria, who spends the entire play eating chocolate (It's a tough role but someone has to do it), Olive who lives like a pig, the vain Amelia, the envious Diane and the lustful Susie. These sinful angels are squabbling amongst themselves when a man enters. This is a female only Celestial Punishment Centre so he shouldn't be here but he's a man and so naturally, despite him being no oil painting, Susie is all over him.

It turns out that this man is also here for punishment. His sexist views have earned him a spell with the women in the hope that they will help him to mend his ways. He seems to know quite a bit about the women but, leaving that aside, arguments soon start to rage about the shortcomings of both sexes. Before long the women have heard enough of his theories about the ability to withstand pain and put matters to the text by giving him a wax.

This is too much for him and he concedes that women are, after all, the superior race and, having learned his lesson, he is permitted to leave – but not before he shocks the women by revealing his identity.

Fallen Angels is a fun play that makes no attempt to be clever or sophisticated but will, nevertheless, be enjoyed by both cast and audience.

FIRST PERSON SHOOTER
Author: Paul Jenkins
Publisher: Nick Hern Books
ISBN NO: 9781848421417
Cast: 3M 1F
Type: Full Length

We are at the SAS training camp in the Brecon Beacons. Captain Jones completes the briefing of his troops then introduces a newbie, Ade, except Ade is not in the Brecon Beacons and neither is Captain Jones.

Ade is in his bedroom playing a simulation game on his computer. As the instructions flash up on the screen Ade's mother, Maggie, enters with dinner, but lure of food, even his favourite pizza, is not enough to distract Ade from his game.

So we know we are in for a play about a mother's relationship with her son. At work she is the manager of Tom, a computer geek, and before long she is confiding in him about her need to connect with her son and he offers to teach her the lingo.

Whilst Tom enjoys shoot 'em up type computer games himself, in real life he is something of a pacifist. So when an IT application that he developed for the rail network is picked up by the Ministry of Defence he is initially opposed to the sale. Meanwhile, in a case of virtual reality becoming reality, Ade is applying to join the army. But things are not what they seem. Ade has learnt that the army uses a simulator to evaluate new recruits and this simulator is about to be released on to the market as the latest must have computer game. Ade wants to steal a march on other gamers by getting in a bit of practice before it even hits the shops.

Back to Tom, and it is no longer the Ministry of Defence interested in his application, but the American military. Maggie is off to the States to do the sales pitch but a last minute domestic crisis - Ade has gone missing - means that Tom has to go in her place. The new computer game is released and it is revealed that Ade has been camping outside the store to buy it. At home he overdoses on the game and ends up in hospital with exhaustion. Tom completes the deal in the US and Maggie loses her job.

The dialogue between Tom and Maggie throughout the play is witty and the changes to their relationship kept me interested. However, the interruptions from Captain Jones within the computer game, although accurate of many a domestic scene, became distracting after a while.

First Person Shooter is well written with believable characters, but nothing very much happens. In the endAde swaps his obsession with games for one for fitness, but I was left with the impression that it is all just part of growing up and he was going to be all right. I was rather hoping for something more dramatic.

DAVID MUNCASTER

FLEA IN HER EAR, A
Author: Georges Feydeau translated by John Mortimer
Publisher: Oberon Books
ISBN NO: 9781849430869
Cast: 9M 5F plus extras
Type: Full length

This classic French farce written around the turn of the last century was translated by John Mortimer for a production at the Old Vic in the mid nineteen-sixties. This edition is published by Oberon Classics following a revival at the New Vic in December 2010.

Raymode Chandebise suspects her husband, Victor, of having an affair and sets in motion a plan to entice him to Hotel Coq d'Or where his misdemeanours will be exposed. The wordplay between Ramonde and her best friend Lucienne is a delight as they decide to write a letter to Victor, from an anonymous and non-existent admirer, asking him to rendezvous at the hotel. When Victor receives the letter he believes that it must have been intended for his friend, Tournel, who secretly admires Raymonde. However, the letter has been written by Lucienne and when Victor shows it to her husband he immediately recognises the handwriting. Come the day of the meeting, all the interested parties arrive at the hotel and, as one might expect chaos ensues.

Modern audiences will be uncomfortable at finding humour in a character's speech impediment but the script does offer scope for playing that down and all the classic elements of farce are here for ambitious companies with the budget for the necessarily elaborate set.

FRANKENSTEIN
Author: adapted by Patrick Sandford
Publisher: Nick Hern Books
ISBN NO: 97818484221943
Cast: 8M 4F + extras
Type: Full length

To say Patrick Sandford's adaptation is true to Mary Shelley's classic novel is a bit of an understatement. In fact every word spoken by the characters is taken directly from the original text which means that the dark atmosphere of one of the greatest horror stories of all time is preserved in this haunting stage version.

We begin on ice as Walton, a polar explorer, heads for the North Pole. In a violent storm his vessel becomes ice-bound and, whilst the ship is immobile, his crew spot a sledge. They drag it aboard and we meet its owner: Victor Frankenstein. As Victor relates his story that led him to the ice in search of the hideous creature that he created there is an opportunity for a director to let their imagination run free. With the action moving from ice-bound ship to sunny Geneva in one scene change, a minimal set is a necessity and I believe this demonstrates one advantage theatre has over other forms of performance. To create a convincing scene through the use of lighting and the other tools available to a director is what makes a night at the theatre a magical experience. Stage directions such as 'enter St George and a dragon' are likely to either excite or terrify anyone asked to produce this play!

With Victor's young brother William murdered and the boy's nurse hanged for the crime, Victor is distraught. Knowing that it is the monster that he created that murdered his brother he determines to find and destroy it.. Suddenly the creature is among us demanding that Victor create him a companion: a female. At first going along with the demand, Victor then relents at the last moment and destroys the life he is creating. In revenge the creature takes another life: that of Elizabeth, Victor's cousin and bride to be. As the story reaches its climax we are back aboard the ice-bound ship where Victor must face the ghosts of those who have died.

At the heart of the story are loneliness and a desire for companionship and this excellent adaption of a classic tale is sure to stir the emotions.

FUNERAL OF MACIE LOVERETT, THE
Author: Gytha Lodge
Publisher: Drama Association of Wales
ISBN NO: 9781898740933
Cast: 6M 7F
Type: One Act

Attached to the back cover of this script is as CD containing a Microsoft Powerpoint presentation. The slides form part of the production which explains the curious statement on the back cover that this is a story that is told, in part, through a variety of fonts. The script also contains lengthy descriptions of the thirteen characters in the prefix and there are yet further instructions as each character enters the action. I feel this is a bit of overkill but at least the actors will be left in no doubt about the type of person they are required to portray.

We start with the first of the slides being projected onto a screen, the text welcoming the audience and giving us an example of the type of humour we can expect. Then the first of Macie's family enters and the bickering begins. In the next scene the slides tell us that it is after dinner and this is where the conversation first turns to fonts: "If you thought in a font what font do you think it would be?" asks Spiro, son of the departed. He thinks he would be Rage Italic. He did consider Rockwell Extra Bold but felt this too straightforward for a complex person such as himself. After some consideration, Lausanne, his sister, settles on Copperplate Gothic Bold. Spiro mocks her: she might as well have chosen Times New Roman!

I assume that the fonts being discussed are supposed to match the slides in the Powerpoint presentation but on my computer they all displayed as Calibri. However, technical issues aside, good use is made of the slides to display the unspoken thoughts as the guests begin to assemble. As the story develops we delve deep into the minds of the characters and their relationships. I became totally absorbed by this odd group of personalities and what they could tell me about the departed Macie. We learn of a life that Macie kept secret throughout her marriage, the reason why her children have such unusual names and that love will always win in the end.

The Funeral of Macie Loverett is consuming, witty and intelligent; a play that would be demanding to perform but well, well worth the effort.

GENTLEMEN AND PLAYERS
Author: Vic Mills
Publisher: Drama Association of Wales
ISBN NO: 9781898740902
Cast: 3M
Type: One Act

Elizabethan England and a playwright, Ben Jonson no less, is improbably imprisoned in a set of stocks. With his head and hands trapped he is at the mercy of passers-by. But not to worry: here is his friend, William Shakespeare. Surely he will soon be free. Unfortunately not. Will seems to have something of a grudge. He is definitely unhappy about something though he does seem to be enjoying this opportunity for revenge. Rubbing mustard on Ben's lips he encourages the poet to think of a simile for burning. The response is somewhat less than poetic.

The dialogue between this pair is an absolute joy. Ribald yet intelligent and very, very funny, the text will have an audience hooked from the first line. There are plenty of Shakespearean references to delight us thespians but a knowledge of the Bard's writing is not necessary to enjoy this play. In fact, I am quite sure that someone who had never even heard of Ben Jonson or William Shakespeare would find this just as funny as the most erudite scholar.

We eventually learn that the reason for Will's displeasure is that he believes that Ben has mocked him in one of his plays but, just as the two protagonists seem to be resolving their differences, the ghost of Shakespeare's father appears to give the story a final twist.

This is a great script which fully deserves to become a favourite at festivals. Thank you, Vic Mills. You've made my day!

GET ONE FREE
Author: Eve Blizzard
Publisher: New Theatre Publications
ISBN NO: 1840944722
Cast: 5F
Type: Full length

A funeral parlour: such a popular setting for plays presented in amateur theatre. We imagine a sombre mood broken by incompetent funeral directors, a missing body, perhaps a ghostly apparition. Thankfully, with Get One Free, Eve Blizzard has created a very different establishment. The impression from the set description is one of a modern travel agent and Furzman Funeral Directors, or at least the grandson of old Mr Furzman, has made a unique offer to clients: Buy One, Get One Free!

To her daughter's consternation, Edie wants to know more about the offer and while she is waiting we learn what an independent old lady she has become. Into the scene comes Winnie, distraught that her great aunt has finally passed on, but frustrated by the fact that the funeral parlour cannot take her booking because the new system is all on young Mr Furzman's computer and he is away at the moment.

Get One Free bobs along at a jolly pace but I thought that the conflicts got resolved rather too quickly and when the precise details of the Get One Free offer are finally revealed it felt neither significant nor funny enough to justify being the focus of the play.

GETTING THE BREAKS
Author: Derek Webb
Publisher: New Theatre Publications
ISBN NO: 9781840947281
Cast: 3M 3F I Male Voice
Type: One act

Getting the Breaks is a one act youth play about growing up: the changes that young people have to face and how they cope with them. There is an element of fantasy in all the characters' lives which ranges from harmlessly dreaming about scoring a maximum break in snooker in front of a worshipping crowd, to more serious delusions that can cause damage to the relationships between friends and loved ones.

Zoe announces that she is pregnant and when Jason gets to hear this news he assumes that he is the father. We sympathise with the position that Zoe finds herself in: Jason is carefree and irresponsible and Zoe feels that this is something she is going to have to deal with on her own. In the end though, it is Jason who takes hold of the situation, separates fantasy from reality and brings normality back to everyone's lives.

This is a play that a young audience would enjoy and the author should be congratulated for creating an educational script that avoids preaching.

GOING TO ALASKA
Author: Tim Kenny
Unpublished: contact branddevelopment@btinternet.com
ISBN NO: None
Cast: 2M 2F
Type: One act

Len is planning to go to Alaska with his best friend Brian for the fishing trip of a lifetime, not that Len's wife, Meg, knows this. She thinks that the pair will be doing their fishing on the Dee, but we get the impression that she is not all that bothered anyway.

We join the couple at their home as they are preparing for Brian and his new girlfriend, Sharon, to come round for dinner. Meg once had a bit of a fling with Brian and, whilst Len is in the dark about this, he is unhappy about the amount of attention his friend pays to Meg and instructs her to wear her dowdiest clothes. Unperturbed, Brian cops a good old feel when he arrives.

As the play progresses it seems clear the way things are heading, but they don't turn out as one might expect. The men are like peas in a pod and soon forget all about the women who, left on their own in the house, find that they have more in common than they might have imagined:they certainly share a lewd sense of humour. When Meg is not using innuendos she is just coming right out with it, and the women form an allegiance which results in an unexpected twist in our tale.

Going To Alaska is an engaging one act play with excellent pace and characterisation.

GOLDFISH BOWL, THE
Author: Joe Graham
Publisher: J Garnett Miller
ISBN NO: 9780853436690
Cast: 1M 2F 2 Voices
Type: Full length

Some years ago I read a news story about a reality TV show that never was. I forget the details but the gist is that a number of contestants were put into Big Brother style house for six weeks and they played to the cameras in the hope that they were carving out a career in TV. Unfortunately for them the cameras were fake. The only bit that was filmed was their reaction when they were told, at the end of the six weeks, that none of their antics had been screened.

The Goldfish Bowl is a new reality TV show in which the contestants must keep a group of goldfish alive in order to win a share of the prize money. As the play begins the three contestants are attempting to create a domino rally, using fish fingers, in order to win the food for their evening meal. Forgetting that the cameras are on them, they talk openly about their reasons for being on the show, then quickly adjust their behaviour once they remember that every word is being heard by the viewers. This joke is repeated several times during this one act play until all is revealed. It seems that viewers have not been voting for their favourite contestant but have, in fact, been voting off their least favourite goldfish!

There are some good moments in this play. I quite enjoyed the fun had with the fact that the fish had been named after the Spice Girls but I fear that this type of reality show, like the Spice Girls, has had its heyday.

GRAVE, THE
Author: Melville Lovatt
Publisher: New Theatre Publications
ISBN NO: 9781840948042
Cast: 2M
Type: One act

In a graveyard Michael is sitting on a bench reading a book. He is a man in his twenties, dressed in denim, with a studious appearance that would give one the impression that he has come to this place for a bit of peace and quiet. This is disturbed by Williams, an older man who is shabbily dressed apart from his brand new shiny shoes.

This is a one act play in the Theatre of the Absurd genre associated with playwrights such as Samuel Beckett. It lurches from extreme violence, to humour, to menace in a manner that is likely to remind the viewer of Waiting for Godot, but the story never strays very far from the real world. Are Williams' shiny shoes stolen and, if so, why should Michael care? Who is Michael anyway and what was the real purpose for him being in the graveyard?

The Grave is open to a multitude of interpretations and is the sort of play that an audience will ponder after the curtain falls. I believe that this makes it well worth considering as a festival entry.

HALF A CROWN
Author: Jane Lockyer Willis
Publisher: Spotlight Publications
ISBN NO: 9781907307232
Cast: 3M 3F
Type: One Act

Maud is a secretary at a firm of solicitors. She is also a princess; something that is obvious from the fact that, as she sits typing her legal correspondence, on her head sits a crown. She has become tired of the royal life: all that waving and smashing of bottles against ships is so tedious, but unfortunately the crown is stuck and this is not the only link to her past she is unable to cast off.

Half A Crown is described as a modern day fairy tale, and so it is - complete with a moral of the story. Maud cannot truly let go of her past until she acknowledges how pompous she has become. Once she does so she is able to remove the crown without any difficulty.

Although I would have preferred the play to have ended half a page earlier before we learn that everything we have just witnessed has been part of a role play, this is an entertaining little romp that will appeal to many groups.

HANDBAG, A
Author: Anthony Horowitz
Publisher: Samuel French
ISBN NO: 9780573052576
Cast: 4M 2F
Type: Short play

Ask any of us theatrical types to say the title of this play and you will almost certainly hear an impression of Dame Edith Evans as Lady Bracknell. A Handbag is, indeed, based around a rehearsal of The Importance of Being Earnest, but this is no community theatre: the young people getting to grips with Oscar Wilde's celebrated script are in a very different place.

When the rehearsal breaks down, the characters become themselves and we realise that we are in some kind of institution and that the script that they are learning is as alien to them as an episode of Midsomer Murders would be to visitors from another planet. What kind of institution is not immediately apparent but what is clear is that George is in charge. He is director, he is playing Jack Worthing, and he is determined that The Play Is The Thing.

What starts out as a comedy turns darker by the minute but there are still some wonderful laugh out loud moments. When the actress playing Lady Bracknell objects to the handbag being made from leather on ethical grounds, George explodes telling her that they are not planning a performance of The Importance of Being a Vegetarian, but then, when questioned on how the play ends, he admits that he does not know. Act Three of the script is missing, the pages lost when the staples were removed. You see, they are not allowed staples in this place.

We are spared from learning specifically what horrific crimes have brought these six people together in this rehearsal, but the world of cucumber sandwiches and muffins on the lawn is in sharp contrast to their daily routine and we are left wondering whether any of them are deserving of our sympathy. This is a thought provoking, short play which will appeal to a teenage audience.

HANGING IN THERE
Author: Geoff Saunders
Publisher: New Theatre Publications
ISBN NO: 9781840947854
Cast:: 4M 3F
Type: Full Length

Ian Lavender, most famous for the role he played in Dad's Army where he became the recipient of Captain Mainwaring's immortal line "Don't tell him, Pike", is the Vice President of the Orchid Cancer Appeal, a charity that does research into Testicular Cancer. Hanging In There is written based on the author's own experiences of the disease, and twenty five percent of profits go to the charity. Contrary to Mainwaring's advice, however, Geoff Saunders has told us everything. This is not a gloomy play, though. Thought provoking, yes, but also very funny.

When we find a subject embarrassing we often turn to humour to hide our discomfort and the author has used this to his advantage in producing a script that has plenty of laugh out loud moments as well as highlighting the issues that many men have acknowledging the risks of the disease. The main character, Jack, is played by two actors who explain in the opening dialogue how the two of them became one: something that, in their eyes, made them half a man. Given the subject matter it is not difficult to identify the part of Jack's body to which they are alluding.

As the play commences the two Jacks take it in turn to play the scenes and narrate which is an effective way of letting us know what is going on in Jack's head as well as providing plenty of laughs as the pair of them behave like squabbling siblings. Jack stumbles upon his wife examining her breasts for lumps and, in the ensuing conversation, she asks him if he ever checks his testicles. The following evening he is in the pub and decides to broach the subjects with his mates looking, no doubt, for some reassurance that it is OK in a man's world to concern oneself with such things. One of his mates, 'Caveman' Dave, would sooner talk about anything else. He is a man's man who thinks all the touchy-feely stuff should be left to the women but Jack's other friend, Howard, is more sympathetic. To Dave this makes Howard Mr Holistic-Green-Party-Get-In-Touch-With-Your-Femininity and it later becomes clear that Dave and Howard have nothing in common apart from being mates of Jack. Following Howard's advice, Jack checks himself in the bath where his body is relaxed, finds a lump and so his journey begins.

The play is described as a comedy and at times it is very funny indeed but the message is clear: if we would only stop skirting around, making jokes and changing the subject. If we just face up to the facts then things will almost certainly not be as bad as we imagine them to be. The recovery rate from Testicular Cancer is already very high but it would be even higher if men got over the fear and, if they suspect that they might have a problem, get it checked out.

I picked up this script intending to take a brief look at it and read it properly at a later date. However, once I started reading I could not put it down. The educational value means that this play would be perfectly at home in schools and colleges but, as a piece of entertainment, it deserves to be in our theatres. This is a very good play which is beautifully written, compelling and satisfying.

HANSEL AND GRETEL
Author: Carl Grose
Publisher: Oberon Books
ISBN NO: 9781849430579
Cast: 4M 3F
Type: Full length

Kneehigh Theatre was established in Cornwall in 1980 and tours throughout the UK. Hansel and Gretel premièred at the Bristol Old Vic in 2010 and is credited as being a collaboration between Carl Grose and Kneehigh Theatre.

Our story begins as a pair of rabbits appear on stage to introduce us to the twins Hansel and Gretel. A cute beginning, but then there is the sound of a rabbit snare going off and moments later Mother appears to announce that it is to be rabbit pie for dinner, holding aloft the main ingredient for all to see. As Father teaches Hansel to chop wood, Mother teaches Gretel to skin the rabbit and we know that we are in for a fairytale with a large dollop of grim reality thrown in. As the search for food becomes ever more desperate, the twins are forced to make a decision. Do they eat their last slice of bread or use it to leave a trail home?

After a bit of a slow start, things pick up in act two when we get to the witch's house and there is some delicious silliness from the character, Birdy. A note in the script at this point indicates that the part was tailored to match the actor's nationality and it is true that the whole script reads rather like a souvenir of the Kneehigh production rather than something to inspire a director to mount their own version of the show. An interesting read but not something I expect to see on many amateur stages.

HEALTHY GRAVE, A
Author: Simon Brett
Publisher: Josef Weinberger
ISBN NO: 9780856763366
Cast: 1M 1F
Type: Full length

Robert and Hilary are in their seventies and have been married for more than forty years. As a university lecturer Robert is used to having an audience, but now he only has Hilary, who puts up with his self indulgent diatribe with an understandable lack of good grace.

For an elderly couple their manner of speaking seems quite youthful and they both demonstrate something of a spring in their step when it comes to extra-marital affairs, his being rather less clandestine than he imagines.

There is a lot of gentle humour in this play and Brett captures nicely the kind of banter that only exists amongst people who know each other very well. The moments of affection feel particularly natural for a couple who have been together for so long: for example, in one touching moment, Robert says "We're all right aren't we?" rather than a more obvious declaration of love.

As Robert's bitterness at not getting the kind of rewards from his career that he believes he deserved is revealed, there are a few heartfelt side swipes at the world of academia and its relationship with the media and, due to the characters being so believable, I could not help feeling sorry for the pair of them: Hilary for the sacrifices she has had to make to support her husband but Robert also, for the deeply hidden knowledge, briefly exposed, that he has been deluding himself for most of his life.

A two-hander is always a challenge but it is refreshing to read a play that offers such rewarding roles for more mature actors.

HI-DE-HI
Author: Paul Carpenter and Ian Gower
Publisher: Samuel French
ISBN NO: 9780573111686
Cast: 9M 8F
Type: Full length

Stage adaptations of popular television comedies seem to be in vogue at the moment. In this last year I have had the opportunity to see Dad's Army, Fawlty Towers, 'Allo 'Allo and Rising Damp. Now, whilst the actress who made Gladys Pugh a nation's favourite tours in Calendar Girls, we are presented with the chance to bring Hi-De-Hi to the stage.

So, to Maplin's Holiday Camp in the 1950's. Gladys plays the notes C G E on her xylophone and yells out "Hello Campers. Hi-De-Hi!" It would be a mean spirited audience that did not respond with a rousing "Ho-De-Ho!" But the play has not started. This is a rather neat prologue that gives Gladys the opportunity to do your theatre's safety announcement: the location of the fire exits, no flash photography and, of course, mobile phones must be switched off.

The play begins and the familiar characters are gradually introduced. I can imagine the delight as the audience recognises each one. Peggy, desperate to be noticed; Mr Fairbrother, bewildered by this unfamiliar world; Fred, stealing sugar lumps for his horse; Ted, the camp comic; Spike, his sidekick and, of course Fred Astaire and Ginger Rogers – or Barry and Yvonne as they prefer to be known.

The story concerns Joe Maplin's announcement that he is setting up a camp in the Bahamas and will need female Yellowcoats to go out there to work. The annual 'Miss Yellowcoat' competition will decide who goes and Gladys and Sylvia go head-to-head. Peggy, meanwhile, is thrilled that whoever wins the resulting vacancy will give her the chance to swap her mop and bucket for a yellow coat.

There are no surprises with this script; if you have seen just one episode of the TV programme, then you will know what to expect. Actors will enjoy impersonating the actors who made the roles famous and the audience will enjoy rating their efforts. As a piece of throwaway entertainment Hi-De-Hi provides a fun evening at the theatre.

HYPOTHERMIA
Author: Vanessa Brooks
Publisher: Josef Weinberger
ISBN NO: 9780856763229
Cast: 3M 2F
Type: Full length

Hypothermia is set in a mental hospital and on the frozen lake on its doorstep in 1940s Germany. Osker is a patient and a favourite amongst the staff as well as the other inmates. He jokes, sings and looks after the plants in the conservatory.

Nominally in charge of the hospital is Dr Erich, but he is barely in control. He refuses to speak to the patients' families and seems more concerned about the plants than the inmates. As he says, he really ought to allow the weak ones to die so that the healthy ones can thrive but, as a doctor, it is his instinct to do his best for all of them. He is, of course, talking about the plants. His administrative assistant is Lisa who is harassed and put-upon but very capable, and there is also Dr Katscher, a charming and athletic man who likes to exercise by swimming between the holes in the ice. Dr Katcher is a member of the SS.

Tension bubbles away under the surface: Dr Katcher seems about to explode with testosterone; Dr Erich is losing control; and then in walks Frau Poppendick. She is the mother of a patient recently deceased and an ardent supporter of the Nazi party.

Knowing what we now know about the Nazi party's attitude toward the mentally ill, and of the experiments carried out in the name of research, the truth about what really happened to Frau Poppendick's son is a nagging concern and, when she returns later in the play to confirm our fears, our attention is concentrated on what is to become of Osker.

Hypothermia is not without humour but, as the story reaches its symbolic climax, it will leave the audience grieving for man's inhumanity to man.

I AM HAMLET
Author: Richard James
Publisher: Lazy Bee Scripts
ISBN NO: None
Cast: 2M
Type: One act

An Am Dram company is preparing to put on a production of what, to many, is Shakespeare's greatest play but, unfortunately, their Hamlet has fallen down the stairs and broken his leg! Needing to re-audition, Tom, the producer, arrives at the theatre to gather his thoughts when in walks Simon who is a newcomer to the area. He is brimming with confidence and very keen to take on the role. The problem is that he does not seem to know anything about the play, or indeed any play or anything at all about the theatre in general. He has seen the film though. Well, he has seen The Lion King which he says is based on Hamlet.

After a while we begin to wonder what Simon is doing there. What started as a funny little sketch about someone totally ignorant of the theatre auditioning for Hamlet, has become somewhat darker. There is menace in the air. What is Simon's motivation? Does he have a connection with Tom? Given the Hamlet connection, the climax of the play may not come as a complete surprise but it is satisfyingly done all the same.

This play requires two very good actors: once Simon gets going his performance as Hamlet should be spellbinding and there are large chunks of Shakespeare that the audience have to realise are relevant to the story. I Am Hamlet is a very good one act play. It is clever and witty and with the right performers it would make a great festival piece.

IF I WERE YOU
Author: Alan Ayckbourn
Publisher: Samuel French
ISBN NO: 9780573111952
Cast: 3M 2F
Type: Full Length

How many times have you used the phrase, "if I were you", without a thought? When we offer advice after opening with those words what we really mean is, "if I were me in your predicament". But what if we actually could become another person, and they you? This is the premise for Alan Ayckbourn's latest publication.

The play begins with the unmindful routine of a family getting ready for the day ahead. Jill is mother and is trying her best to stir her husband, Mal, from his slumber whilst attempting to get some breakfast into their son, Sam, before he departs for school. The pressures of the day begin for Mal even before he is dressed. His phone rings: it is a staff member calling in sick. Things can only get better – but they probably won't. Mal is not the only one having to deal with frustration. For Jill it is the little things, Mal leaving the toilet seat up, for example, that cause her to voice her irritation whilst she doesn't even mention the more important matters – such as the fact that she is aware that her husband is having an affair.

Mal is the manager of a furniture showroom where he works with his daughter's husband, Dean. As the scene changes from Mal's home to his workplace we see a bit of what makes Ayckbourn such a genius. The furniture showroom is identical to the house with areas for sitting room, kitchen, bedroom and bathroom. Only the lighting changes to indicate the change of setting. This means we can flit between the shop and the house in an instant so the action never stops.

As one would expect with Ayckbourn there are large dollops of pathos along with the laughs: Jill's confession to her daughter, Chrissie, that the love has gone out of her marriage; her knowledge that Mal is having an affair; the unexplained bruises on Chrissie's arms. These all help to give the text a multi-layered quality as we get drawn into the lives of these ordinary people who are also extraordinary.

The extraordinary bit comes right at the end of the first act when Mal and Jill swap places overnight. Physically they both look the same, it is just their personas that have changed places and, as they try to come to terms with this, the audience has the interval to imagine the consequences.

People swapping personalities has, of course, been done before but in If I Were You Alan Ayckbourn does it very well indeed. As Mal and Jill do their best to carry on they each realise that they can learn a lot from the other and they can also learn a lot about themselves by being someone else. In the end they both change back to their old selves but we are left knowing that things will never be the same again.

For me, If I Were You is the best script from Ayckbourn in years. Audiences will love it and anyone lucky enough to be cast as Mal or Jill will find their role challenging but fantastically rewarding.

IMPERIAL FIZZ

Author: Brian Parks
Publisher: Josef Weinberger
ISBN NO: 9780857633403
Cast: 1M 1F
Type: Full length

A 1930s Art Deco apartment. Melodies play from a classic RCA radio whilst a couple straight out of the world of Noel Coward sing, dance and exchange witty banter. His tuxedo, her cocktail dress are just perfect and the slightly tipsy conversation is delightful and clever. They chatter away as they await a special guest, but all is not what it seems.

From the off we know something is wrong, but we don't know what it is. What dark secret lies in sharp contrast to their world of comfortable upholstery? This is the tension that lurks in the background as we enjoy the intelligent bickering.

The script is peppered with sophisticated exchanges such as:

Woman: I wish I could sing as nicely.
Man: It's a pity no one has yet invented the notes you use.
and
Man: You say things behind friends' backs.
Woman: I admire their shoulder blades.
Man: You have flirted with men at parties I did not attend.
Woman: Absence makes the heart go wander.

As they discuss their lives together they adopt the personae of different characters to give evidence as though they are on trial, taking it in turn to be prosecutor, defendant, judge and jury. Eventually we come to realise that, for this couple, life is over. The special guest? The grim reaper, perhaps, but in the end comes disappointment as it seems that the afterlife, like life, does not quite come up to expectations.

Imperial Fizz is a challenging play both for the actors and the audience. As it is a two hander, both actors have a lot of lines but the real difficulty lies in maintaining interest. The introduction of different characters will help but it would be a shame if the audience missed the meaning due to losing concentration. However, done well, this is a play that will be discussed in the bar long after the curtain falls.

IT FELT EMPTY WHEN THE HEART WENT AT FIRST BUT IT IS ALRIGHT NOW
Author: Lucy Kirkwood
Publisher: Nick Hern Books
ISBN NO: 9781848420816
Cast: 2F
Type: Full Length

Dijana is Eastern European and a victim of the sex traffic industry. She is in her flat waiting for the next client. This will be the twenty second today and, she believes, the last one ever. She looks nice, her hair freshly washed with shampoo that she has stolen from Boots the Chemist: L'Oréal. Because she is worth it. As it happens, she knows exactly how much she is worth: Babac, her pimp/boyfriend, paid one thousand euros for her, and the next client will earn her the £30 she needs to give Babac the twenty thousand pounds to buy her freedom.

Dijana is a victim, but she is a survivor and an eternal optimist. As we go on a journey through her mind it is at times heartbreaking, at times surreal, and at times very funny. One gets the impression that Dijana doesn't want our sympathy, she just wants us to understand and this challenging piece of theatre has the potential to change people's attitudes toward the industry in which she is trapped.

Lucy Kirkwood wrote 'it felt empty' whilst working as the playwright in residence at Clean Break, an organisation that works with women who are, or have been, in prison and has used the experience to construct a play that gives us a sense of what it is like to live in captivity. As you would expect with a play about this subject, there is strong language and adult scenes throughout.

JOSEPH K
Author: Tom Basden
Publisher: Nick Hern Books
ISBN NO: 9781848421547
Cast: 3M 1F
Type: Full length

Tom Basden first came to public attention as the author of Party; a play recently reviewed in this column. It won an award at the Edinburgh Fringe Festival, transferred to the West End and was adapted for Radio Four. However, though it was entertaining enough, I found it rather unmemorable. Joseph K is an altogether different kettle of fish.

As we begin Joseph K, his surname is just the single letter, is drying himself following a shower. There is a knock on the door and, expecting it to be the take-away sushi that he ordered, he calls out for them to come in. The man who enters is, indeed, holding a box of sushi, but he isn't the delivery man Joseph K was expecting. In a hesitant and mystifying opening scene we learn that the man with the sushi is Gabriel and that he and another man, Nathan, are there to arrest Joseph K.

Based on Franz Kafka's 1925 novel The Trial, the play transfers the action to twenty first century London but loses none of the dark comedy of the original. Two days after the men with the sushi incident Joseph K is back in the bank wondering if it was all a wind up. But if it was why can't he use his mobile phone, why doesn't his passport work and why is he limited to withdrawing only £20 at a time from a cash machine? As the story unravels we encounter many of the annoyances of modern life such as unhelpful help centres and being automatically charged for services we have not used and useless self help software. The scene where Joseph K tries to use a virtual lawyer, Andrew Martindale, is very funny and we will all identify with his frustration. Eventually Joseph K gets to see a real lawyer but he turns out to be about as useless as the computer program and, as things begin to spiral out of control, logic goes out the window.

Tom Basden clearly had a lot of fun writing Joseph K and this comes through in the text. The surreal nature of the work on which this play is based is fully evident and we eventually reach the point where we join the title character in questioning whether anything we have witnessed is real or imaginary.

JUST THE TWO OF US
Author: Ros Moruzzi
Publisher: Samuel |French
ISBN NO: 9780573121449
Cast: 1M 6F
Type: Short play

Matt is struggling to write a novel. Ruth is his understanding wife and breadwinner. The two of them are portrayed as a happy, loving, and supportive couple. However, they don't seem very much like real people due to the unsubtle scene setting which requires the pair to have conversations that people in real life just don't have. The comedy is also disappointing: ploys such as being rude on the telephone before realising it is your partner's mother - a mother who is bemused by mobile phones and who thinks lasagne is a Chinese dish give the play the feel of a rather tired TV sitcom.

However, things do pick up with the arrival of Karen and her daughter Freya, who claims that Matt is her biological father, and the play benefits from the arrival of more characters and the quickening of the pace. The action really does hot up with the arrival of Bev, wittily described as Freya's tummy mummy but, sadly, the humour seems to dry up towards the end and all we are left with is tantrums and accusations.

Just the Two of Us is good in parts but, despite its contemporary storyline, is rather old fashioned.

THE KISS
Author: Melville Lovatt
Publisher: New Theatre Publications
ISBN NO: 9781840948035
Cast: 2M 1F
Type: One act

Simon observes his wife and his best friend locked in an embrace. The kiss is long, passionate and highly inappropriate. Simon is convinced that they must be having an affair and plans a terrible revenge.

Physical harm is what he had in mind, but circumstances prevent him from carrying out the horrific attack he had intended. Instead, he relates a dream, the violent undertones of which are not lost on his friend.

We never know for certain whether the affair ever took place but The Kiss is notable for what is left unsaid. It is a one act play that packs a punch and, like all the best thrillers, will leave the audience guessing long after the curtain goes down.

LA BÊTE
Author: David Hirson
Publisher: Nick Hern Books
ISBN NO: 9781848421141
Cast: 5M 5F + Extras
Type: Full length

La Bête was first published in New York in 1991 and this new, updated version has been released by Nick Hern Books to coincide with the

2010 West End revival. As I write, the play is currently wowing them on Broadway with Joanna Lumley playing a role that had originally been a male part.

Set in France in 1654, the play takes the form of rhyming couplets, delivered at such a pace that the audience are left with little choice but to immerse themselves in the performance.

"Challenging" is the word the word that springs to mind when thinking of the poor actors who play the main roles. The script runs to one hundred and twenty four pages and that is an awful lot of words! One character, Valere, makes his entrance with an unbroken speech that goes on for a full fourteen pages. Does the fact that it all rhymes make it easier or more difficult to learn, I wonder?

The story concerns Elomire, head of the Royal Theatre Troupe. His princess has deemed that the court ensemble admits a member: the outrageous troubadour, Valere. Not only that, but she insists that they must perform one of his ludicrous plays. Elomire is incensed but must accept his patron's decree with all the good grace he can muster. He persuades his princess that Valere's play, "The parable of two boys from Cadiz", be presented as an ensemble piece rather than a monologue. He believes that this will expose Valere as a fool but his plan backfires when his troupe find that they rather like the play. The princess, though troubled by some unflattering references to France, eventually comes down in favour of Valere and Elomire is forced to leave the troupe.

This is a play that is all about language. It is clever without being highbrow. It treats the audience with intelligence but it is still accessible. It is absurd and at the same time entirely believable. A serving maid who only speaks words that rhyme with 'blue' seems perfectly in place in the most unusual royal court. Challenging, certainly but anyone brave enough to take this on would surely find the experience most rewarding.

LAST REEL, THE
Author: Ron Pearson
Publisher: Jasper publishing
ISBN NO: 9781905993574
Cast: 5M plus voices
Type: Full length

It is Christmas Eve. We are in Yorkshire and it is snowing outside, but we are cosy and warm in the barn conversion. No roaring fire though.

Jack Quarmby has all mod cons including underfloor heating and a TV that recedes into the wall at the touch of a button. As the play begins Jack is happily watching the closing moments of Casablanca on said TV and, once that has ended, is just choosing a Laurel and Hardy DVD when his friend Greg arrives. Greg is on the brink of being promoted to Detective Inspector in the local constabulary and it is clear that Jack is a firm family friend, so it is intriguing that when Jack has a telephone call and then a visitor, neither of which he seems happy to receive, there appears to be a suggestion of a somewhat murky past.

The truth is that Jack is a happily retired assassin who is being badgered by two old associates to do 'one last job' – each other – but Jack is too much of an old movie buff, and knows that doing one last job inevitably leads to being caught. However, once both of them are in his house, he knows that he is going to have to make a decision, whether he likes it or not.

Jack is an amiable enough character, and there are plenty of amusing lines, but I feel that The Last Reel would benefit from a bit less back story and a bit more tension between the two adversaries.

LATE MIDDLE CLASSES, THE
Author: Simon Gray
Publisher: Nick Hern Books
ISBN NO: 9781848421103
Cast: 4M 2F
Type: Full length

The Late Middle Classes was first published in 1999 after winning the Barclays Theatre New Play Award for its première production directed by Harold Pinter. Despite the accolade the play failed to make it to the West End but a revival at Donmar Warehouse has resulted in this new edition being published by Nick Hern Books.

The play is set in the 1950s where Holliday is a twelve year old boy beginning his journey of sexual discovery. His mother, Celia, accidentally stumbles across him in his bedroom on his knees holding a naturist magazine and asks the boy's father to have the talk that every father and son must have. The subsequent vague and stuttering conversation is indicative of both the times, and the distance between the pair.

Whilst Holliday's father is distant, his mother is suffocating, insisting that the boy tell her that he loves her, not just because she is his mother but in a 'special way'. Meanwhile, the boy's piano teacher, Mr Brownlow, harbours desires for his pupil and engineers to be alone with him.

However, Brownlow is not depicted as a seedy child abuser. Like the boy's mother, he is frustrated by the austerity of fifties Britain and is seeking an outlet for his longings. His childish games with the boy are inappropriate, but stop a long way short of exploitation; though we are left to imagine, with horror, how things might have turned out if Holliday's father had not put a stop to the lessons.

The Late Middle Classes is a beautifully understated, thought provoking drama that fully deserves its recent revival.

LIFE IMITATES ARTIST
Author: S. W. Senek
Publisher: www.productionscripts.com
ISBN NO: none
Cast: 3 not specified
Type: One act

Life Imitates Artist is a short play in which three painters seek to achievethe notoriety of the recently deceased Vincent Van Gogh. They have already each cut off an ear and they are now deciding which of their number will take his own life; thereby allowing the other two to benefit from having been associated with the tortured artist. Artist A has, literally, drawn the short straw but he is none too happy about it, whilst the others try to persuade him to do the honourable thing.

There is plenty of Three Musketeers type silliness, with paintbrushes in place of swords, and the play is entertaining throughout. However, this said, the ten minute play market is rather saturated, particularly in America, and I don't feel that Life Imitates Art is exceptional enough to make it stand out.

LILIES ON THE LAND
Author: Sarah Finch, Dorothy Lawrence, Kali Peacock, Sonia Ritter,
Natasha Tamar and the Lions part.
Publisher: Nick Hern books
ISBN NO: 9781848421134
Cast: 4F plus doubling
Type: Full length

Lilies on the Land came about when the Lions part theatre company
were looking for a play that echoed the wartime experiences of women.
Realising that they knew little about the part that the Women's Land
Army played in World War II, they wrote to Saga Magazine asking
for their readers to send any material they had. They received nearly
one hundred a fifty letters from former members of the Land Army
containing stories, poems, photos and newspapers cuttings. The
resulting play is understandably anecdotal in nature but still makes an
interesting and entertaining piece of theatre.

The stories are told through four characters: Margie is a pretty, childlike
doll of a girl from Newcastle who struggles working alone on a farm.
Peggy is a cheerful cockney who didn't know one end of a cow from
another before falling in love with the countryside, and Jim - the farm
foreman. Poppy comes from a privileged background but soon earns the
respect of the farm hands through her willingness to get stuck in. Vera
is probably the most complex of the characters for whom the war is an
opportunity for her to discover who she really is. All the characters are
based on real life persons interviewed as part of the process of creating
this play.

As we progress through the timeline the girls recover from the shock
of the new: the filth, the cold, the toilet behind the hedge until they
become both competent and confident. There is tragedy, of course, but
on the whole it is an uplifting play that does a lot to remind us of the
huge contribution to the war effort that was made by these girls in the
fields.

LINGUA FRANCA
Author: Peter Nichols
Publisher: Samuel French
ISBN NO: 9780573112287
Cast: 3M 4F

Turn to the Show Diary in Amateur Stage Magazine and there is a good chance that someone, somewhere, will be performing Privates on Parade, Peter Nichols nineteen-seventies musical farce that was a huge stage success and a slightly less successful film. In Lingua Franca the playwright has taken one of the main characters from his earlier work, Steve Flowers, and transported him to nineteen-fifties Florence where he is attempting to teach English in a rather chaotic language school.

As the play commences Steve is teaching his first class and struggling to keep them under control. He loses his patience and insults his students: a mild insult by English standards but his class is horrified. They refuse to be taught by him any more and Steve is told he no longer required. But the Italian manager doesn't sack him. He is likable and, though there are plenty of English teachers looking for jobs, he gets another chance. This is partly due to fellow Brit, Peggy, who takes Steve under her wing, though he is more interested in Heidi, a newcomer from Munich.

The play is described as 'sexually charged' and this comes not only from the characters on the stage but also from unseen budding Gina Lollobrigidas in the classroom. Time and again Steve is warned about his conduct but in the end it is not him that oversteps the mark. Tension comes from Heidi's deep seated prejudice against Jews and she clashes with the anit-fascist manager and Russian Jew, Irene: but Steve is blinded by lust, ignoring the smitten Peggy in favour of the playful Heidi.

Lingua Franca is an intelligent play. The classroom scenes provide plenty of humour and the staff room represents the cosmopolitan disorder of post war Europe. This is Peter Nichols first play in a decade and is a fine addition to his catalogue.

LITTLE PLATOONS
Author: Steve Waters
Publisher: Nick Hern Books
ISBN NO: 9781848421516
Cast: 6M 5F
Type: Full length

In the run up to the general election in 2010 the Conservative party put a lot of faith in their vision of a 'Big Society' which empowered people to take control of matters at a local level. Little Platoons is set in August of that year and is an examination of how the Big Society might work in practice. Rachel joins a group of like-minded parents who want to set up a free school outside of the state system with the ambition of giving their children an education that is both effective and enjoyable. A big ask that needs big ideas, and Nick is the big personality who thinks he can bring it all together.

The play begins at Rachel's house where Martin, her ex, is sorting through a box of books whilst the pair discuss their attempts to find a decent school for their son, Sam. There is an undercurrent of distrust and one-upmanship typical of a couple that have recently split up but, nevertheless, the conversation is mostly good natured. Then Martin drops a bombshell. He and his new partner are moving out of London and he has the answer to the question of how to best serve Sam's educational needs. Sam will move out with them.

The thought of losing her son is the catalyst Rachel needs to make her do something about her life and her son's education. She goes to see Nick, whose vision for a free school is based around his rather discordant ideals rather than conforming to the national curriculum, and she soon falls for his charms. So, when he suggests that she give up her job at a state school to become his head teacher, she is flattered into finding the suggestion irresistible.

The themes of Little Platoons: Coalition Britain, The Big Society and People Power make it a very contemporary play; but that could be its undoing. Already some of the narrative seems out of date and some of the lengthy pieces of dialogue about the issues facing people who work in the teaching profession will not have universal appeal. However, the play is well written and I expect we will be hearing much more of Steve Waters in the future.

LONDON ROAD

Author: Alecky Blythe with music by Adam Cook
Publisher: Nick Hern Books
ISBN NO: 99781848421769
Cast: 6M 5F + extras
Type: Full Length with music

London Road in Ipswich was, until a few years ago, known to locals as the red light district. The Neighbourhood Watch Association tried, for a long time, to get the girls off the streets but then, in 2006, a series of shocking events changed things for ever. The bodies of five prostitutes were discovered and Steven Wright, the occupant of number 79, was arrested, charged with and then convicted of their murders. The media frenzy that followed the story catapulted the other residents of London Road into the spotlight and their experiences are captured in this play that made its première in 2011.

As the bodies were being discovered there was an inevitable excitement at being the focus of the national news but also horror at what was happening on the doorstep. The local radio station gave away panic alarms but, as one resident pointed out, unless you were a prostitute there wasn't really anything to fear.

The script was developed through a series of interviews and the text is in local dialect with much of the dialogue being sung. As it takes us through the time line of the door-to-door enquiries and the arrest, trial and conviction of the man described by his neighbours as a simpleton, we get a sense of the community coming together until it culminates with prizes being award for the London Road in Bloom Competition.

It is an unusual piece of theatre but I feel that the involvement of the authors in the development of the play is so important it would be difficult for any other company to consider it as a production.

LOVE AT LAST

Author: Raymond Hopkins
Publisher: Hanbury Plays
ISBN NO: 9781852053291
Cast: 3M 7F
TYPE: Full length

Love at Last is set at the Autumn Glade Retirement Home which is occupied by a mixed bag of elderly residents. Frank and Rose are a married couple with a working class background. Frank was nicknamed Swannee when he was younger because, as a shop steward at a car factory, he caused more strikes than a box of Swan Vestas. His nemesis is Helen, described as a well educated snob, persuaded to enter the home by her two sons after her husband had died.

Within the first few pages of the script everyone seems to have told us their life stories, which is a little unnatural, but necessary as the subsequent action requires us to know the characters that we are dealing with. Things start to go missing. First it is Frank's lighter, then a watch and then a necklace. Suspicion falls on the new care assistant, thoughsome of the audience may fall for a rather neat red herring early on in the script. The care assistant is innocent and it seems that Frank, himself, may be the culprit, but with love in the air everyone is acting a little strangely.

Finding plays with older casts can be a bit of a challenge but, with seven of the characters over seventy, Love at Last is a play well worth considering.

LOVE THE SINNER
Author: Drew Pautz
Publisher: Nick Hern Books
ISBN NO: 9781848420892
Cast: 10M 2F + Doubling
Type: Full length

Some plays begin with a bang. Love The Sinner begins with an explosion! A heated debate is mid flow around a hotel conference table, somewhere in Africa, as a group of bishops discuss regime change. The cacophony is halted with the arrival of coffee and things become slightly surreal as the delegates close their eyes tight shut so as not to see the waiter. They are supposed to be sequestered and must have no contact with the outside world until they make a decision. This means that no one sees the waiter, a young African called Joseph, except Michael, a lay delegate accompanying the bishops.

Joseph is a member of The Holy Mountain of Fire Mission to the World and has to take tremendous risks just to go to worship. Such devotion inspires Michael and in the next scene we are with the pair in his hotel bedroom where the men have had a sexual encounter. What follows is a very uncomfortable conversation which hints at blackmail after the act that has just occurred . Joseph wants Michael to help him get to England claiming that his life is at risk.

Back in Britain, Michael's life begins to unravel. He has squirrels in the attic, he is unable to get his wife pregnant and his growing obsession with religion is unsettling his wife and alienating his work colleagues. When Joseph arrives, uninvited, Michael is forced to face up to the consequences of his own actions.

Love The Sinner is an uncompromising play which is at times shocking, but never ceases to be plausible and thought provoking.

LOVE'S YOUNG DREAM
Author: Ros Moruzzi
Publisher: J Garnet Miller
ISBN NO: 9780853436560
Cast: 4M 4F
Type: One act

Avril and Trevor are preparing for a family gathering. Their daughter, Jill is going to marry Peter and they nervously await the arrival of their future son-in-law's parents. Apparently, they haven't spoken for years so the meeting promises to be difficult but when Peter's mother and father each arrive with new partners it is time to fasten your seatbelts: we are in for a bumpy ride.

The introduction of so many characters so early in the play can lead to an audience becoming confused as to who is who, but Ros Moruzzi's characters are so well defined it should not be a problem in this case. The two mothers have very different views about the forthcoming wedding but Avril insists that there is no point in discussing it until her daughter arrives. Unfortunately, she never does arrive for a very good reason – as Peter eventually explains – she has called the wedding off.
In the second scene the two mothers are at it again. This time we are in a maternity ward, Jill having just given birth, and the argument this time is about the baby's name and who is going to be 'Nana'.

Love's Young Dream is a fast paced, accessible and funny one act play with characters that seem all to familiar.

LUISE MILLER
Author: Friedrich Schiller adapted by Mike Poulton
Publisher: Nick Hern Books
ISBN NO: 9781848421479
Cast: 7M 3F
Type: Full Length

Ferdinand is in love with Luise Miller. He is the son of a Chancellor: the chief minister to a German prince and the most powerful statesman in the land. She is the daughter of a humble court musician and marrying outside of one's class just isn't done in 18th Century Germany. A further complication is that Luise is pursued by another man; the appropriately named Wurm, who Luise's father sums up rather well describing him as a "civil-servile, rat faced, writ scribbling pox blister". Wurm lives up to his reputation by telling the Chancellor of Ferdinand's affection and intentions towards Luise.

Ferdinand proves himself to be a fool. He falls for a scheme, hatched by Wurm, that forces Luise to write a love letter to another man in order to free her father from prison where he has been locked up for defending his daughter. Ferdinand seems destined to marry instead Lady Milford but although her ladyship herself declares that 'a play must have a happy ending', it is not to be. In a sense I was quite satisfied that Ferdinand paid the price for his lack of faith in his young love but it is impossible not to be moved by the sad fact that the innocent must suffer along with the guilty.

A tale of seduction and political manipulation, Mike Poulton's adaptation is, at times, quite wordy by modern standards but feels as contemporary as the television programme The Thick Of It. Despite being in five acts, the overall running time will suit modern audiences and the story certainly packs a punch.

LYSISTRATA – THE SEX STRIKE
Author: Germaine Greer and Phil Wilmott adapted from Aristophanes
Publisher: Samuel French
ISBN NO: 9780573112591
Cast: 8M 11F
Type: Full length

Athens is at war with Sparta. It seems as though the futile conflict will drag on until everything is destroyed, but one woman is not prepared to allow that to happen. Lysistrata calls on the women from both sides to take matters into their own hands: they will go on a sex strike until peace is declared.

The women gather in the bathhouse, a place that is strictly men only, and Lysistrata reveals her plan. Much of the language is very bawdy, and the humour quite basic, but one does get rather swept along by it and I can imagine an audience enjoying carry-on-esque lines like 'I need a stiff one'. Being convinced of the need to take such drastic action, the society women leave the bathhouse to be replaced by the Senators and Secret Police. Now is the opportunity for the cleaning women to come into their own, provoking the men into a state of anger before Lysistrata and her clan return to flaunt their bodies and tease the men until they are, well, "overcome". The tables are turned and it is now the women who will sit in judgement as Lysistrata reflects that peace, at every level, is less damaging than war, and it is men's insistence to revel in the glory of war that causes the most damage.

The action becomes even more earthy in act two, probably making the play unsuitable for many amateur groups, but despite all this raunchiness the best features of the script are the moments of poignancy and Greer has not shied away from reminding us of the tragedy of war. It is debatable whether Aristophanes himself would have approved of the pacifist message contained in this adaptation but much Greek theatre is very relevant in today's world and this is a perfectly (in)decent adaptation.

MAKING MONEY
Author: Terry Pratchett adapted by Stephen Briggs
Publisher: Samuel French Limited
ISBN NO: 9780573112645
Cast: M19 F10. Extras
Type: Full length

It is twenty years since Stephen Briggs first brought Terry Pratchett to the stage when the Studio Theatre Club in Abingdon produced Wyrd Sisters. This first play was a massive hit and has become a favourite amongst amateur theatre groups. Since then Briggs has become known as an authority on the series of Discworld novels having written books about the series as well as his many stage adaptations.

In Making Money, Moist von Lipwig is employed as the Postmaster General of the Ankh-Morpork Post Office but is forced into taking over the running of the Royal Bank. Finding that people trust banks much less than they trust the post office he uses his skills as a former con-man to change the way money is valued, with the currency being supported by the city rather than gold. The story could hardly be more topical and it is a tribute to Prachett's perspicacity that his novel was published in 2007 before the real life banking crisis became apparent to us ordinary mortals.

The play opens with a speech which is almost word for word the same as the beginning of an episode of Ronnie Barker's Porridge and this will, perhaps, reassure audiences unfamiliar with Pratchett's work that they will be able to relate to the action on the stage. Indeed Ankh-Morpork is a fantasy world that so closely resembles our own that the characters seem both ridiculous and familiar at the same time. With so many adaptations available, any society deciding that they want to stage one of the Discworld plays are rather spoilt for choice but, with Making Money, timing may be the thing that is of the essence.

MAKING THE GRADE
Author: Peter Hartley
Publisher: Drama Association of Wales
ISBN NO: 9781898740971
Cast: 2F
Type: One Act

India and Jasmine are sisters, refugees from a war in Africa, now living in Britain. Their chances of being able to remain in the country are dependent on India getting the teaching job for which she is having an interview this morning. Unfortunately, as she is severely hung-over, there is no possibility of her keeping the appointment. A pretty serious situation but the women's bickering is typical of siblings and very funny.

Jasmine is, in fact, furious. The plan was that, as the younger of the two, she would enrol as a student on the Performing Arts course that India would be teaching. But then Jasmine has an idea: she will attend the interview pretending to be India. By the time term starts in September no one will remember what she looks like and India will be able to start the job.

Everything goes exactly according to plan except for one small snag. Jasmine gets the job but they take her photo for the ID card. This means that when term starts the sisters are forced to continue with their deception and, although it is all rather far-fetched, it is easy to get carried along by the story. India becomes disillusioned with the job – the job that Jasmine is actually doing – and decides there is more to life than just handing out grades, especially in an establishment where the management have decreed that each of the students will get top marks at least once. India decides to go back to Africa, where she believes education has more value, meaning that the sisters will have to swap their identities for the rest of their lives.

The script has a good deal of warmth and humour. The dialogue leaps of the page and is littered with sibling squabbles and very strong language but we also get one or two glimpses into the horror that the girls have left behind in their homeland; the references to their 'imaginary mother' all the more poignant for not being fully explained. Every so often I read a script that I really want to see performed and this is one of those times. If you have a suitable cast and are looking for a strong festival piece I would urge you to consider Making the Grade.

MAM
Author: Allan Williams
Publisher: Drama Association of Wales
ISBN NO: 9781898740919
Cast: 2M 2F

A family living room: Peter enters and has the kind of conversation that he has been having with his mother for the last forty years. She still treats him like a child, asking if he has had a good day, checking that he has taken his shoes off and filling him in on all the local gossip. He takes it all in good humour though he does have the odd mutter under his breath when he wants to say something but daren't let his mother hear. It is a scene of comfortable domesticity but things take an unusual turn when Peter's ex-sister-in-law enters the room. It is as though Peter's mother is no longer there which is, in fact, just the case. They buried her this morning.

I thought this was going to be a play about a son unable to cope with the loss of his mother but there is actually much more to it than that. There is sibling rivalry and unrequited love but, essentially, this is a story about human frailty, love and kindness. It is a heart warming and thoughtful one act play with a satisfying ending that leaves us pondering what lies in store for the characters.

ME, AS A PENGUIN
Author: Tom Wells
Publisher: Nick Hern Books
ISBN NO: 9781848421042
Cast: 3M 1F
Type: Full length

Stitch has left the stifling small town atmosphere of his home in Withernsea to stay with his very pregnant sister, Liz, and her husband in Hull. Here he has met Dave, a gay friend of his brother-in-law, and become a bit infatuated with him. As an excuse to see him again, Stitch takes his nephew to the aquarium where Dave works and, as a treat, they are allowed to feed the penguins. As the play begins Stitch is explaining to his sister that she cannot use the bathroom because their nephew fell into the penguin pool and is now having a bath to warm himself up. Then the phone rings and it is their nephew on the line, so he can't be in the bathroom. In that case why doesn't Stitch want anyone to go in there?

Kidnapped penguins aside, this is essentially a play about growing up. Liz and her husband are having to adjust to the idea of becoming responsible parents, whilst Stitch is on a steep learning curve as he dips his toe into Hull's gay scene. Me, As A Penguin is a very funny play with some brilliantly funny lines, but it is also tragic and thought provoking. I believe that Tom Wells is a young playwright that we will see a lot more of in years to come.

MEDEA
Author: Tom Paulin from the original by Euripides
Publisher: Nick Hern Books
ISBN NO: 9781848420946
Cast: 3M 5F plus chorus
Type: Full length

A married couple spilt up. He has given into lust and the chance to do a bit of social climbing. She is left with the kids. Punished for something that was not her fault she extracts a terrible retribution. This is the synopsis of Medea which earned Euripides third place in a playwriting competition in Athens two and a half thousand years ago. Actually, only three playwrights entered the competition so, in effect, Euripides came last. Since then, Medea has become a most popular Greek tragedy featuring, as it does, one of the strongest female roles in the history of theatre and has been adapted many time into many different forms.

Shortly after Medea takes the stage she is ordered to leave the city of Corinth by the king, who happens to be the father of the woman that Jason, Medea's husband, is now planning to marry. She begs him for one more day in the city to make her plans, and her wish is granted. As the king leaves she vows to 'turn their marriage into darkness', and 'blacken the day they chose to banish me'. She makes a fool of the king of Athens, the city where the play was first performed, then sets about her murderous revenge.

Northern Broadsides toured with this version of Medea early in 2010 to mixed reviews but I found the script compelling, modern and accessible.

MICKY SALBERG'S CRYSTAL BALLROOM DANCE BAND

Author: Ade Morris
Publisher: Samuel French
ISBN NO: 9780573112911
Cast: 2M 1F
Type: Full length

It is 1952 and Polish immigrant Micky Salberg and his daughter Sam are just about surviving on their small farm on the outskirts of Stoke-on-Trent. As the play begins Micky is serenading his pig, a sad lament about the problems of non- productive cows, whilst Sam is out in the farm yard. Her long coat is covered in pig muck and there is nothing feminine about her appearance. Tommy enters. He is a young Stoke lad who claims to have been attracted by Micky's song and their short dialogue quickly establishes their characters. Sam seems very confident but vigorously hides her femininity. Tommy is a cocky teenager acting, and pretending, to be older than his real age and someone who speaks without thinking, or even caring, about the consequences.

Tommy is sent on his way and Sam enters the farmhouse to berate her father. The bailiffs are due any moment, the gas is about to be cut off and all he can do is get drunk and sing to his pig. But Micky has news. He has got them a gig at The Crystal Ballroom in Burslem and he just needs Sam to agree to sing. She refuses but does agree to play the clarinet. The night of the gig and Tommy appears, suggesting to Sam that the addition of his guitar would 'fatten' up the sound. It seems that Tommy is a bit of a virtuoso, but more than that, thanks to his father's collection of jazz 78s, he has heard of Micky Salberg. Micky is surprised. He was known in the dance halls of Krakow but did not expect to be recognised by someone from the home of coal, steel and the toilet bowl!

Micky's relationship with his daughter and her relationship with Tommy provide plenty of opportunity for both humour and pathos. The three characters are beautifully observed and as the play progresses we begin to regard them as friends and we are willing them to succeed. However as act one comes to an end, we learn a surprising bit of information about the bailiffs and find that Tommy is about to be conscripted into the army.

Act two and Micky has plans to keep Tommy at home and the band together but this, unfortunately, involves Tommy marrying Sam and starting work on the farm. This is not something that is met with universal approval but, putting the problem to one side for now, the band switches to playing rock and roll and they really take off. When it comes to the time for Tommy to leave to do his basic training we expect him not to go, but leave he does, though the play does end with a very satisfying twist.

Warm, thought provoking and very funny, Micky Salberg's Crystal Ballroom Dance Band requires three multi talented actors but the challenges of production are worth overcoming in order to bring this peach of a play to the stage.

MOMENT
Author: Deirdre Kinahan
Publisher: Nick Hern Books
ISBN NO: 9781848421523
Cast: 3M 5F
Type: Full Length

We are in the Dublin home of Teresa, a sixty year old widow, whose daughter, Niamh, is fussing because she tried to telephone her mother and got no answer. The reason for this is that she had been out to the supermarket to buy quiche for tea. She is expecting a special guest: her son, Nial.

With the arrival of a second daughter, Ciara, we soon realise that this is a family for whom division and sibling rivalry is the norm, but one thing the two daughters do seem to agree on is the dismay at the news that their brother is to pay a visit. However, blood is thicker than water and so they agree to be present in order to please their mother.

When Nial arrives he has a surprise in the form of his new bride, Ruth. Things are fairly polite to begin with but Ruth causes a storm when she explains that she is aware of Nial's "history". So far this has been the story of a family doing their best to get along with each other but now we learn the reason for all the underlying tension. Nial's "history", as Ruth calls it, is that he has done time for murder, and the victim was Niamh's best friend, Hilary.

The problem for me is that it has taken far too long for us to get to this revelation. We must be well over an hour into the play and, to be honest, I was starting to wonder when anything significant was going to happen. After the interval we go back in time to meet Hilary, a happy mischievous child who Nial smothered with a pillow when her teasing pushed him over the edge. Then, back in the present, we further explore the effect that this one moment of madness had on an ordinary Dublin family.

As a study into how people try to get on with their lives by avoiding the subject that is never very far from their thoughts Moment works quite well. However I fear that many audiences will find it difficult to maintain their interest when there is so little happening on the stage.

MONEY MAKES YOU HAPPY
Author: Francis Beckett
Publisher: Samuel French
ISBN NO: 9780573023880
Cast: 3M 4F
Type: Short play

Jeremy is a writer. Well, he wrote a book once but he hasn't really produced anything in years. He is idealistic and a bit of a dreamer. He worries about things that most of us would never think about. Ruth is practical, neat and tidy, organised; a woman who knows what she wants and how to get it. They haven't got a thing in common; apart from the baby that is.

Jeremy's shock when, on a surprise visit to his former girlfriend's home he discovers that he is a father, sends us on a comic journey as he forced to confront the realities of the world of business and politics. His determination to take his responsibilities as a father seriously sees him having to make a choice between principles and cash.

I suspect that most of us have met the kind of people that Jeremy is forced to deal with and Beckett's script pokes fun at them with relish.

Money Makes You Happy is a cheerful little play; it is witty and moves along at a fair old pace and it is all so good natured that you hardly notice the little digs at the world in which we live. There is depth, though, and a happy ending that is sure to please.

MORTE D'ARTHUR
Author: Adapted by Mike Poulton from Sir Thomas Mallory
Publisher: Nick Hern Books
ISBN NO: 9781848420953
Cast: 15M 6F
Type: Full length

Thomas Mallory's epic tale of the Knights of the Round Table was first printed in 1485. Said to be England's first 'best seller', it comprised twenty-one volumes of often incomprehensible prose which Poulton himself describes as a rambling page turner. His task, therefore, was one of interpretation and selection in addition to adaptation. The resulting stage play was first performed by the Royal Shakespeare Company at Stratford upon Avon in 2010 and is now available for amateur theatre companies who are fortunate to have a plethora of young men.
We begin with the pulling of the sword from the stone and this is followed by the establishment of the round table, the quest for the Holy Grail and, finally, the death of the king. I don't know the running time but at 115 pages I can be certain that an audience would be in for a long evening. The sprawling adventure, with Lancelot and Guenever's love story thrown in, has seventy-five named characters with dialogue that is sometimes a peculiar mix of ancient and modern.

Mike Poulton is acclaimed for his adaptations and he must be congratulated for making sense of this monster, but I'll admit that I did find it rather hard going and felt that he might have been even more selective about what to include. Either that or adapt the tales into two or even three plays. It would certainly be an ambitious director on the amateur or professional stage who considered taking on a production of Morte D'Arthur.

MOTHER CAME TOO
Author: John Waterhouse
Publisher: New Playwrights' Network
ISBN NO: 9780863194801
Cast: 2M 2F
Type: Full length

Although Mother Came Too is published by New Playwrights' Network it must be said that John Waterhouse is a bit of an old hand. In fact this play first saw the light of day on television in 1965 starring Peggy Mount and, I am afraid, it is somewhat showing its age.

A pair of newly-weds are setting up home in their council house. (Do you see what I mean?) The groom's mother has come along, not just to wish them well but also to live with them, as the saying goes, hilarious results.

Except it isn't really hilarious and, though there has been some attempt at updating the script – I don't believe they had car boot sales in the mid sixties, any contemporary references seem at odds with the style of the piece. There is a certain charm about it as one considers how different things are in this day and age but I fear there is very little for a modern audience to relate to in this play.

MOVING ON
Author: Richard James
Publisher: Lazy Bee Scripts
ISBN NO: None
Cast: 1M 2F
Type: One Act

Users of the English language should celebrate that their chosen tongue affords them the luxury of phrases such as 'moving on'. Adulterous footballers, grieving parents, politicians who fiddle their expenses and unsuccessful candidates on The Apprentice can 'move on', the implication being that, regardless of whether they are guilty of any sin, it is now time to put it behind them, forget about it and concentrate on the future. In some other languages, Japanese for example, there is no direct translation of this meaning of the phrase and so the native speakers are destined to live with the consequences for ever.

In Richard James' play it is Angela who is moving on, but she has no reason to reproach herself. She has lived a guiltless life and was married for forty years to a man whose recent death has prompted her to leave the family home with all its memories and start a new life in a small flat. As Angela packs the final few items into tea chests her daughter tells that she has asked a family friend, Bob, to help with the transport. Angela is horrified and we wonder if she is as innocent as she appears. What dark secret could be lurking behind the tears? With Bob's arrival we learn the truth and I was relieved to find that the author, resisting the temptation to tarnish Angela's reputation, allows his play to remain a touching and affectionate account of love, loss and moving on.

MRS AFFLECK
Author: Samel Adamson
Publisher: Samuel French
ISBN NO: 9780573112898
Cast: 5M 4F 4 Other
Type: Full length

Henrik Ibsen's Little Eyolf debuted in Berlin in 1895 and tells the story of the Allmers and their disabled son, the Little Eyolf of the title. His disability arose when he fell from a table as a baby whilst his parents were too busy making love to care for him. Samuel Adamson's adaptation moves the story to 1950's England: The Allmers are now Rita and Alfred Affleck and their son is Oliver; the Rat Woman of the original is replaced by 'Flea', an enigmatic and charming teenage boy, but the substance of the tale remains, as does the unusually affectionate relationship that Alfred has with his half sister, Audrey.

Alfred is something of a dreamer: he writes poetry and reads Shakespeare to his son, but whilst away in Scotland he began to see things differently and has decided he is now going to devote himself to Oliver. Flea visits the house and asks if there is anything bad that they want rid of, but he is sent away. After this Rita's jealousy of the attention Alfred lavishes on Oliver and Audrey leads to an argument during which Oliver leaves the house. Once again his parents are too busy to care for him and he makes his way down to the sea where he drowns. Audrey's discovery that she and Alfred do not, after all, share the same father leads her to believe that they have a future together but, in the end, it is Alfred and Rita that are reconciled.

Ibsen is celebrated for the challenges to Victorian values and morality that characterised his dramas: Adamson's adaptation attempts to modernise the story by making Rita the centre of the action, but it left me with a feeling that I would rather just watch the original play.

MUM'S THE WORD
Author: Susan J Bevan
Publisher: Drama Association of Wales
ISBN NO: 9781908575067
Cast: 3F
Type: One Act

Susan J Bevan's first play was Half a Million Women which was an autobiographical story of a fifteen year old forced to give up her child for adoption. When the play was first performed the author sat in the front row with her daughter with whom she had been re-united only that afternoon. The media interest catapulted her to fame and a writing hiatus lasting nearly twenty years followed.

Now back writing and performing Susan J Bevan has produced another play about motherhood; this time looking at it from a different angle.

Jane and Sophie are sisters. Both are hitting forty and, whilst Jane has two teenagers and another child on the way, Sophie chose her career over being a mother. Now, however, her biological clock is ticking and nearing 12 o'clock.
The script rapidly takes us through Sophie's pregnancy and the birth of her child. She experiences for the first time that feeling that most parents have: loving someone so much that their life is more precious than your own. So how, she wonders, could her own mother have walked out on her and Jane?

Their mother is Miriam who, ironically, gives lectures on motherhood at a university. Sophie decides to contact her – Jane has been in touch for years – and, after an awkward start learns the truth about her mother.

It was guilt that made Miriam leave: Guilt at being a bad mother and guilt at being a bad daughter. As Sophie learns about her mother and grandmother she realises that the version of events that she grew up with is far removed from reality.

Powerful though Mum's the Word is, I don't feel that it quite works as a play. Miriam has some very long speeches and it would perhaps be better if some of her past were played out rather than just talked about.

MY WONDERFUL DAY
Author: Alan Ayckbourn
Publisher: Samuel French Limited
ISBN NO: 9780573113048
Cast: M2 F3, 1 girl (aged 9)
Type: Full length

My Wonderful Day is a play told through a child's eyes. Whilst the author acknowledges the difficulty in find a child who is, or at least looks, nine years old it is such an essential part of the story that it will just not do to 'age up' the child to, say, fourteen and have a seventeen year old play the role. The play must be told from the perspective of a nine year old.

The child in question is Winnie the daughter of the second generation Afro-Caribbean Laverne who is heavily pregnant. As the play begins the mother and child have arrived at the house of Kevin Tate, a minor TV celebrity, where Laverne is employed as a cleaner. Winnie is off school, supposedly ill, and is told to sit quietly and do her homework: an essay entitled My Wonderful Day. This particular day, being a Tuesday, is a day in which she must speak entirely in French in preparation for Laverne's dream of moving the family back to Martinique. As Winnie sits and quietly gets on with her work the scenes acted out in front of her give her plenty of material for her essay.

The first visitor is Tiffany, Kevin's Personal Assistant and mistress. We learn of their affair when Tiffany tries to distract Winnie from the argument that Kevin is having with his wife on the telephone in the next room by playing a corporate video that Kevin has just made for some awful sounding resort. The cheesy music is interrupted by the voice of Paula, Kevin's wife, explaining in no uncertain terms the relationship her husband enjoys with his P.A.

Then there is Josh. Summoned by Kevin to discuss the situation with the videos and, in a scene that is both cringingly embarrassing and very funny, the pair talk openly in front of Winnie in the mistaken belief that she does not understand English. Then Laverne's waters break and, whilst she is whisked off to hospital, Winnie has to stay in this strange house until a family friend can collect her. Josh is instructed to look after her but, in a reversal of their supposed roles Winnie reads aloud from her book and Josh falls asleep.

Finally Paula arrives and is briefly maternal until she realises that her husband is upstairs, in bed with Tiffany. The pivotal scene in the play is pure farce, as the naked mistress is thrown out of the house and the cheating husband is brained by his wife's BAFTA; but it wouldn't be Ayckbourn if there wasn't any pathos and this is provided by the fact that this very adult situation is witnessed and recorded by the nine year old child.

NIGHT I DANCED WITH CYD CHARISSE, THE
Author: Nancy McPherson
Publsiher: Spotlight Publication
ISBN NO: 9781907307249
Cast: 3M 2F
Type: One Act

Set in a garage workshop The Night I Danced With Cyd Charisse is the story of three mechanics: Wilson, McBride and Lennox. Their workplace banter reveals a certain degree of companionship though I doubt if they would describe themselves as friends. Wilson, the oldest of the three and the most experienced both in life and in the complexities of the internal combustion engine is given to the odd fantasy to disguise the sadness and loneliness that exists in his life. This is something that he shares with the others and, as the story unfolds, we find that the characters have more in common than at first it might appear.

In the end Wilson has one more tale to tell. When he is called into the office he is expecting a pay rise but when he returns he announces that he is to take early retirement. He tells the others that this has been planned for some time but we know this is not true.

Nancy McPherson's one act play has plenty of pathos and we can relate to and sympathise with the characters. In addition to the men there are two contrasting females who add to the comedy and make the whole thing gel. I enjoyed reading this script and would recommend it as a festival piece.

OH MY GOD
Author: Daniel Sossi
Publisher: Drama Association of Wales
ISBN NO: 97801898740940
Cast: 3M 11F
Type: One Act

Oh My God was written by an English playwright whilst living in Belgium, is published by a Welsh publisher and was first performed in

Germany. All this is appropriately cosmopolitan for a story about the omnipresent being.

The play starts with great reverence. Gregorian Chant music fades and, as the lights come up on a monastery interior, the sisters are at prayer. A voice-over sets the scene: whilst researching a historical bible legend a monk finds a secret, the discovery of which means that God himself (or herself) will soon be visiting the monastery. God is himself (or herself) dismayed at this prospect. He (or she) now feels that it was a mistake to put the message in the text. Now all his (or her) good work will be undone. But an angel convinces him (or her) that the people will be overjoyed to see him (or her) and God resolves to show the world just how great he (or she) really is. Back at the monastery there is a theft, then a murder and God and the angel arrive during an argument started by an incompetent detective but all is well once the reasons for the crimes are revealed.

Oh My God is a good ensemble piece but I don't think that it quite lives up to its potential. It is a funny concept and there are a few visual gags but I feel that the dialogue lacks humour.

OH, TO BE IN ENGLAND
Author: David Pinner
Publisher: Oberon Books
ISBN NO: 9781849430562
Cast: 3M 2F
Type: Full length

Oh, To Be In England was written in 1975 but did not receive its première until Mel Cook produced it at London's Finborough Theatre in 2011. David Pinner's reputation for provocative, emotive writing was established when he wrote the novel, Ritual, whilst appearing as the lead in The Mousetrap in the West End. The novel was later made into the cult film, The Wicker Man, starring Edward Woodward.

His plays include The Teddy Bears Picnic: another that was written in the nineteen-seventies but was not performed until decades later. It was considered unproducible when it was first written due to its uncompromising view of Stalinist politics and, if the notes on the back page of the script are to believed, Oh, To Be In England was lost due to the play's representation of nineteen-seventies political extremism. It occurred to me that, with the current economic client and with the

British National Party winning seats on councils and in the European Parliament, this could be a play that with a disturbingly contemporary feel.

With Britain in economical meltdown, stockbroker George Hampton's behaviour has become increasingly erratic until his predilection for speaking his mind earns him the sack. His wife, Kay, is desperately trying to keep the family together as George has a flirtation? with neighbour Antonia; one that is jealously observed by teenage son Rob. In order to help make ends meet Kay takes in a lodger, Florian, who is a handsome and successful German businessman and, in the resulting sexually charge atmosphere, Kay finally tells George to just get on with consummating his relationship with the neighbour. Unable to go through with it George slashes his wrists in an act that was probably more about seeking attention than a deliberate attempt to end his life.

What we have, then, is a play about relationships. George ends up alone, his neighbour having taken up with his son, and his wife with the lodger. The politics, the miners' strike and the rise of Thatcher, provide the backdrop to George's disintegration but are not the essential part of the story that one might expect. Whilst Oh, To Be In England is diverting enough, it is not the lost masterpiece that the back page notes would have us believe.

ORANGES ON THE BRAIN
Author: Joe Graham
Publisher: J Garnett Miller
ISBN NO. 97808533436720
Cast: 1M 1F 1 voice
Type: One act

As the play begins one would be forgiven for thinking that one was watching a version of Frankenstein: thunder and lightning, a low table with a white sheet over it covering what looks like a body and Thea, distraught and screaming to the gods, "No! Not me!" Suddenly the atmosphere changes, the lights come up and Duncan, Thea's husband, enters. He whisks away the white sheet to reveal not a grotesque life form, but several bowls of fruit.

This is a very atmospheric beginning to a comedy about a serious subject. Duncan has a brain tumour, the size of an orange, though we don't discover this until some way into the play. To start we have a good deal of entertaining marital banter as Duncan, much to his wife's annoyance, has dragged out the Smoothie maker and is determined to create the perfect Smoothie. This explains the fruit on the table, not to mention the splashes all over the walls. However it isn't long before the thunder and lightning start again and Duncan turns into a pain-riddled creature obsessed with The Creator. Though Duncan doesn't claim it, Thea believes herself to be this creator. The monster is the brain tumour and it started ten years ago, when she and Duncan first met. But she also believes that, if she created it, then she can destroy it.

Oranges On The Brain is a challenging play in many ways. There are scenes of almost slapstick humour, such as the trying on of hats when each character adopts the persona of a typical wearer of the selected headgear, but the frequency with which they switch from comedy to nightmarish imagery makes the play slightly uncomfortable viewing. This is not a bad thing: theatre should provoke and Oranges On The Brain does it very well.

OUBLIETTE
Author: David Foxton
Publisher: Samuel French
ISBN NO: 9789573121883
Cast: M6 F9, plus 5 M or F
Type: Short play

In a twelfth century manor house stands a room with no doors or windows. This is an Oubliette, from the French 'to forget' and it is the place where our story is set. A tour guide leads a group of visitors into the room via a door recently installed by the trust that now owns the property. As the guide speaks they are all unaware of the ghostly presence of Anne, a servant girl from the past. The guide tells the visitors that the original purpose of the room is unknown, whilst the interjections from Anne, heard only by the audience, add to the mystery.

The visitors leave and the room is filled by more characters from Anne's era. It seems that the Oubliette is something of a den for thieving servant girls, stealing linen from their masters.----- When Anne's master learns of this the girls are quick to blame witchcraft, claiming they were forced into participating in crime against their will.

The master seeks to protect the girl accused of being a witch and we realise that the master's fate and reason for the room being sealed, trapping Anne eternally within the walls, has more to do with greed and ambition than it has with witchcraft.

For a play lasting only around twenty minutes or so, Oubliette is remarkably atmospheric and succeeds in having a satisfyingly complex and intriguing plot.

OUR NEW GIRL
Author: Nancy Harris
Publisher: Nick Hern Books
ISBN NO: 9781848422230
Cast: 1M 2F 1boy
Type: Full Length

Daniel is 8 years old. He is alone in his kitchen at the dead of night. He applies Dettol to his ear then takes a sparkling Sabatier knife from a rack on the wall. There is a sharp blackout just as he appears to be about to slice his ear off.

Two weeks later and Daniel's mother, 7 months pregnant Hazel, is talking to a stranger in her kitchen. This is Annie, a nanny from Ireland who has apparently been appointed by Hazel's husband, Richard, who is currently away with work in Haiti. Hazel is saying that she is sorry but there must have been a mix-up. She doesn't need a nanny. But Annie says that it isn't a mix-up. Mix-up implies some error on the part of Annie or her agency. This is a misunderstanding between Hazel and her husband. Annie has a contract.

Annie stays and, at first, she seems like a godsend. Hazel has given up a career as a lawyer in order to start up a business importing olive oil but she doesn't seem to be doing very well for customers. The oil keeps coming from Italy and the house is slowly filling up with bottles of the stuff. She is so distracted by this she seems to have little time for Daniel and Annie smoothly slips into the void that exists between him and his mother.

It is Daniel who notices that something doesn't seem right. "Annie writes in a notebook", he tells his mother, "I think she writes about you." With Richard back home we learn that Annie is his response to Hazel's cry for help: a practical solution to her being unable to cope. But she didn't want a practical solution – she wanted Richard.

A story of disconnections, Our New Girl is a very dark play that offers just enough comic relief from the angst of modern parenting. Unusually the only character likely to elicit any sympathy from the audience is Daniel. He may be a troubled child but when his father shouts and bawls at him for telling lies when everyone, his father included, knows he is telling the truth it is little wonder that he has behaviour problems.

PARTY

Author: Tom Basden
Publisher: Samuel French
ISBN NO: 9780573122026
Cast: 4M 2F
Type: Full length

A garden shed. Four young idealists have decided that they are going to save the world and are arguing over their policies. They are in favour of China, whatever that means, but are in difficulty when trying to decide their policy toward Muslims. Wishing to avoid causing offence they decide it is probably best just to leave it at 'There are a lot of them in Bradford', except they agonise over whether the use of the word "them" is offensive in itself.

Tom Basden's comedy was a huge hit at the Edinburgh Festival before transferring to the West End and then becoming a four part series in the comedy slot on BBC Radio Four. These four nice but dim young adults attempt to get their small minds round the big issues but get bogged down by the minutiae and it is all too easy to get sidetracked, particularly when there has been the promise of lemon drizzle cake and it has failed to materialise.

Party is nicely written and has plenty of laughs but I felt it lacked originality. The petty squabbling and earnestness greatly reminded me of David Tristram's Last Tango in Little Grimley and the comedy of a committee being unable to reach any decisions was done so well by Alan Ayckbourn in Ten Times Table.

It is perhaps appropriate that the story doesn't really go anywhere. By the end the party still doesn't have a name, still doesn't have any policies and there has still be no sign of any cake. Unlike his protagonists I doubt if Tom Basden is trying to change the world with his play, rather he is just trying to provide an hour's worth of easy-going entertainment, and he does that well enough.

PETER PAN
Author: Andrew Hawcroft
Publisher: Spotlight Publications
ISBN NO: 9781907307164
Cast: Variable Cast
Type: Pantomime

Andrew Hawcroft's pantomime is quite faithful to the traditional story of Peter Pan but, as is customary, has plenty of contemporary references to make it relevant to a young audience. Songs are not included but their nature, and when they should be sung, are included in the script.

To begin with I found the script rather lacking in humour and, when it did come, it could have parents cringing: little ditties about words that rhyme with bucket, for example. However, once we get going, there is plenty to make the audience chuckle, the dialogue between Nana and Captain Hook being the highlight.

Pantomimes are an ideal opportunity for societies to consider work by less well known authors, but it is a competitive market and this script, despite one or two nice moments, lacks anything to make it stand out from the crowd.

PIECES
Author: Hywel John
Publisher: Nick Hern Books
ISBN NO: 9781848421110
Cast: 1M 2F
Type: Full length

Jack and Beatrice are twin brother and sister whose parents have recently died. They have no grandparents, aunts, uncles or cousins: a fact that they explain in a rather laboured fashion to Sophie, their Godmother in the first few moments of the play. Sophie has been away; she hardly knows the children as she hasn't seen them since they were very young, but now they are going to have to get to know one another rather quickly.

The script instructs us that the children must be played by adults so, as a result, we do not know the precise age of the children. They are old enough to make themselves beans on toast, but not old enough to know the difference between fasting and eating fast. On the other hand, some of the words that they use make them sound very grown up and they are, as Sophie points out, nearly as big as their parents. When they appear wearing their parents clothes, talking and behaving like adults, this is just the start of a disturbing twist in the tale. Gradually Jack begins to take control, humiliating Sophie and revealing his knowledge of past events.

Pieces is full of black humour and is an interesting début from this actor turned writer.

PINEAPPLE
Author: Robert Messik
Publisher: Samuel French
ISBN NO: 9780573121982
Cast: 1M 1F
Type: One Act

Now then! Either there is an error in this script or, when this play was first presented at Arundel Festival in 2006, the character of Peter was played by an actress, whilst his wife, Jill, was played by an actor. No matter; regardless of any unintentional gender reversal, our couple live in a comfortable, Ikea furnished flat in North West London. As Peter arrives home he is on his mobile phone ordering a pizza. He carefully establishes the exact time with the person on the other end of the phone, as he plans to take advantage of the fast food establishment's half hour rule. Not delivered in half an hour – the pizza comes free.

Pregnant Jill is surprised by Peter's arrival which is earlier than usual. She has packed her suitcases, written her farewell note and was just about to walk out the door. The naive Peter mistakes the reason for her having her coat on and goes to turn up the heating. When Jill finally manages to get through to him that she is leaving we realise that he knows this, but is in denial.

The dialogue that follows is a kind of verbal ping-pong as they discuss their relationship, her pregnancy, pizzas and the traffic on the A1. Just when we feel that there may be reconciliation in the air, the pizza arrives (two minutes late) and everything is turned on its head.

Pineapple is an excellent play for a one act festival. It keeps it simple, but is engaging, and has the kind of ending that will give the audience something to ponder in the bar after the show.

PLAGUE OVER ENGLAND

Author: Nicholas de Jongh
Publisher: Samuel French
ISBN NO: 9780573113390
Cast: 10M 1F
Type: Full length

A play that takes as its central story line Sir John Gielgud's conviction in 1953 following an arrest in a public toilet might, at first glance, seem to have a minority appeal, but with Plague Over England Nicholas de Jongh has succeeded in writing something of interest to both mainstream and gay theatre. Any fears that this might be a worthy but dull look at the prejudices so prominent in our society just a generation or two ago are soon dispelled as de Jongh's witty and lively script takes us straight into the action. This takes place over many scenes in many locations and most of the actors are required to play multiple roles.

The stage directions are of a most precise nature. I know that a lot of directors like to ignore stage directions in order to put their own stamp on a production, but de Jongh has put a lot of effort into describing how certain lines should be delivered and how characters should look and behave. I believe that the author is, in this case, justified in going to such lengths. Anyone considering producing this would be setting a play in a world that most of us would find difficult to imagine in this day and age, so the help provided by the author would be vital to a successful production.

The first act plunges us into the world of narrow minded judges and politicians, police traps and underground scenes, and culminates with Gielgud's arrest and conviction. Portraying well known real life characters is never easy but de Jongh does it with ease. Gielgud and Dame Sybil Thorndike come across as naturally as Terry the police officer and Greg the young man who tries to come to Gielgud's defence.

Following his conviction Gielgud is portrayed as being ashamed of his action. He is seen to be openly gay amongst his friends but never in public and is said to have told his mother that the arrest was just a misunderstanding. The scene that I had expected to come at the end of the play actually comes fairly early on in Act Two. Gielgud's dramatic first appearance on the stage following the media frenzy over his arrest is neatly done and we are then whisked forward, first by two years, and then by another twenty. It is now 1975; Gielgud has been cast as a gay character in a play by Harold Pinter and he still fears how the public may react to the role following the events of 1953. We do end on an upbeat note, however, when he is taken back to the scene of his disgrace and he finally seems to come to terms with the public awareness of his sexual orientation.

The publicity that surrounded Gielgud's conviction eventually paved the way for reforms and the eventual de-criminalisation of homosexuality and, although Gielgud never publicly associated himself with any gay rights movements, it was revealed after his death that he had donated financially to Stonewall, the campaigning organisation. The public loved Gielgud regardless of his sexual orientation and the audience clapped and cheered his first appearance at The Haymarket following his conviction. It is perhaps fitting that he should be the subject of a piece of gay theatre that has been such a massive mainstream hit in the West End and is now available for amateur performance.

PLAYING WITH MY HEART
Author: Shaun Prendergast
Publisher: Samuel French
ISBN NO: 9780573052606
Cast: 6M 4F with doubling
Type: One Act

We are at the base of The Angel of the North with a bunch of school kids who do not want to be there – obviously. They would much rather be running out of the school gates to start the weekend but they are stuck here on this stupid project.

Geordie, or Mr Pride to the kids, is the jovial teacher trying his best to drum up some enthusiasm whilst his class just want to know when the bus to take them home is going to turn up. One of the girls, Ella, addresses the audience directly to provide little snippets of information that make sense of the somewhat chaotic dialogue typical of a situation where a teacher is just failing to maintain order. Matters are not improved when Geordie has to tell his class that the bus has been held up for at least an hour.

The fragile good humour is shattered and the pupils dredge up old antagonisms as they squabble and become ever more disruptive until the Angel herself has had enough and comes to life to teach the class a few home truths.

Playing With My Heart is an entertaining little play which should be popular with teenage performers.

PORT OUT, STARBOARD HOME
Author: Richard James
Publisher: Lazy Bee Scripts
ISBN NO: None
Cast: 4M 3F + extras
Type: Full length

At one time only the very rich could afford to go on a cruise. It is, of course, the title phrase that gives us the word posh but you no longer need to be posh to indulge in a cruise holiday. Richard James' choice to set his play upon a boat gives him a marvelous opportunity to throw together a number of characters who are unable to escape each other's company, regardless of how much they would like to get away from one another.

Sadly, the characters all seem to be caricatures. There is a camp fitness instructor; an overpowering mother desperate to find a wife for her timid son; a hypochondriac constantly swallowing pills provided by her domineering husband; and a minor celeb recently split from her footballing partner. None of them seem like real people, their dialogue mostly a vehicle for as many puns as can be levered in as possible.

The plot, such as it is, concerns the barman making a play for the hypochondriac and the overpowering mother attempting to get her son off with the celeb. The big laugh to end act one is the son shouting to the celeb in a noisy bar that he is gay. The music ends unexpectedly and his 'confession' (the author's word) is heard by all. I thought that the author might redeem himself when act two gets underway with a conversation between the two gay characters, but any hope disappeared with a pun about turning the other cheek. Eventually the hypochondriac realizes that there is nothing wrong with her, thanks to a remarkably quick diagnosis by the ship's doctor. She also realizes that her husband has been feeding her Smarties in order to manipulate her and the play ends with her running off with the bar man.

I wish I could find something encouraging to say about Port Out, Starboard Home but I am struggling to find any redeeming features. The two dimensional characters and quantity of puns give it a pantomime feel but it is nothing like as much fun. Maybe the humour based around sexual preference is supposed to be ironic but, if so, it didn't come across to me. Surely theatre has moved on from this sort of thing.

PRECIOUS LITTLE TALENT
Author: Ella Hickson
Publisher: Nick Hern Books
ISBN NO: 9781842421660
Cast: 2M 1F
Type: Full Length

Sam is a nineteen year old American sitting on a New York roof top on Christmas Eve. Joey, an English girl, joins him and they awkwardly introduce themselves whilst, between their dialogue, Sam addresses the audience directly, filling in the background and telling us what he is thinking. The next scene is a flashback to earlier in the evening and we see Sam working as a carer for the elderly George. We then replay the first scene but this time from Joey's perspective.

After this the timeline follows a more conventional format and on Christmas Day Sam arrives at George's apartment to start work but, for once, the old man doesn't want him there. The reason is that he has a guest who turns out to be Joey. And Joey turns out to be George's daughter.

We are witnessing the beginning of a love story, one in which the young lovers are determined to make their mark on the world around them. However it is the world that makes a mark on them and they are forced to learn the lesson that George learned long ago: life is what happens when you are making other plans.

It is a credit to the writer that we become close to her characters and want their dreams to come true but the tragedy of the situation is summed up when Sam tells Joey that he loves her and her response is, "That's not the point." Precious Little Talent is uncomplicated on the surface but it digs deep into life's big frustrations and is written with great style. I feel that we will be hearing more from Ella Hickson.

PREPARE TO MEET THY TOMB

Author: Norman Robbins
Publisher: Samuel French
ISBN NO: 9780573113598
Cast: 4M 6F
Type: Full length

When Norman Robbins wrote A Tomb With A View thirty two years ago he couldn't have imagined how popular the play would become. In fact, typing the play title into a search engine on my computer results in no less than 36000 matches. It is no surprise then that the author received many requests to write a sequel. But how do you do that when you have killed off most of the characters? In nineteen-ninety-eight Robins came up with the answer with Tiptoe Through The Tombstones. This had a whole new load of oddball members of the Tomb family gathered in the library at Monument House for the reading of yet another will. We now have the final instalment with just two remaining Tombs running the Monument House and Alternative Health Farm.

As night falls, and the fog inevitably descends, Hecuba Tomb and her niece, Drusilla, receive a series of visitors. There is Sir Beverley Cornstock, on the trail of Drusilla's double-crossing grandmother. Then there is novelist, Phillipa, and her assistant, Daphne, who fear that they are being followed by the notorious 'Norfolk Strangler'. Robert and Miranda, are a pair of honeymooners, and Quentin Danesworth, a TV historian. For all these unexpected visitors their first mistake was to seeki refuge in Monument House, their second was to start asking too many questions.

This is the sort of thing that Norman Robins does best: eccentric characters; secret panels; plot twists that are every bit as shocking, and frequent, as the violent deaths suffered by the cast list;   and a gloriously funny sense of the macabre throughout. He may not be pushing any boundaries but Prepare To Meet Thy Tomb is all jolly good fun and is bound to be a popular choice amongst theatre groups.

PRESCRIPTION FOR MURDER
Author: Norman Robbins
Publisher: Samuel French
ISBN NO: 9780573113383
Cast: 3M 4F
Type: Full length

Prescription for Murder is a rare thriller from the pen of an author more associated with farces and pantomimes. Of course, all the best thrillers have their fair share of humour, just as every comedy should have an element of tragedy and the assured comic touch of Norman Robbins is present here.

The play was apparently written in 2008, yet it seems a little dated in places. There are videos rather than DVDs and, apart from a brief reference, nobody seems to possess a mobile phone. However, the problem doesn't just lie with the props; the language and the way the plot develops give the play the feel of something written twenty or thirty years ago. Of course, it is entirely possible that Norman Robbins set out to write an old fashioned thriller, and I am sure that this will be popular with many audiences.

The story concerns Barbara Forth who is not a well woman. Fortunate then that her husband is a doctor. Or is it? Early on all the clues point in one direction and from our perspective things don't look good for Dr Forth. In fact, there were times when I wanted to shout at the other characters, 'Its him! Can't you see what he is doing?', but Robbins is far too good a writer for it to be that obvious and, when the final revelation comes, it is really rather satisfying.

Overall, despite its old fashioned feel, this is a good little thriller that I expect will prove to be a popular choice with amateur theatres.

PRICE OF EVERYTHING, THE
Author: Fiona Evans
Publisher: Nick Hern Books
ISBN NO: 9781842421493
Cast: 1M 2F
Type: Full length

Eddie is a former barrow boy turned millioneur entrepreneur who lives in his Cheshire manor house with his ex-Beauty Queen wife and their confident teenage daughter.

The three of them have returned from a charity auction where Eddie has just paid £7000 for a large signed photograph of Kerry Katona, much to his daughter's disgust. At just fifteen, Ruby is already familiar with the way the world works and she doesn't entirely approve, but she does have a generally good relationship with her father; one that he can afford to fund.

This is a special weekend. Eddie has taken some days off work, turned off his mobile and has even had the old wedding video transferred to DVD. He announces that they are all going on holiday the very next day, the dog has gone into kennels and he wants to have a nice family evening playing Monopoly. Pam, Eddie's wife, is worried. What is it all for? What is going on? Eddie's behaviour becomes ever more erratic and, when Ruby jokes that someone is prowling around the yard, he goes ballistic. As the first act draws to a close the audience is left in no doubt that something has gone seriously wrong in Eddie's life.

Act Two and everything is much calmer, but the relative peace does nothing to disguise the horror that we just know is bubbling away under the surface. Eddie is continually being caught out as he tells lie upon lie and it gradually dawns on us that the threat to the family does not come from outside the house, but within.

The use of CCTV in this play helps give it the impression of a TV drama, unsurprising as the author writes extensively for television, but The Price of Everything is an entertaining thriller that provides a very strong part for a talented junior.

RAGGED TROUSERED PHILANTHROPISTS, THE
Author: Robert Tressell adapted by Howard Brenton
Publisher: Nick Hern Books
ISBN NO: 9781848421073
Cast: 10M 2F
Type: Full length

Robert Tressell was a painter and decorator who died almost penniless in 1911. Three years later his account of the lives of the men he worked with was published. He had tried and failed to get his manuscript published during his lifetime and it was left to his daughter to present it to her employer after overhearing him in a literary conversation. A much shortened version was published. The full text was not published until 1955 by which time the story of the philanthropists, poor working men lining the pockets of their rich employers, had already had a huge impact on the labour movement and workers rights.

The play begins in the present. Kirsty, an estate agent, is showing prospective buyers around a large Victorian house known as The Cave. She tells them that it was renovated in 1904 but has remained virtually untouched since then. One of the buyers strips away some wallpaper to reveal paintings underneath, at which point Owen appears. 'I did those paintings', he tells her, 'in nineteen hundred and four.' and we are transported back to find a team of men hard at work on the refurbishment. One of them, Bundy breaks into song and the others join in, except for Owen. He does not approve of the song. It is a Tory song, a capitalist song, designed to keep workers in their place.

Wisely, Howard Brenton has shown confidence in Tressell's original story and has concentrated on creating a piece of theatre without compromising the impact of the original text. Owen is initially an outsider, mocked and distrusted by the very people he wants to liberate, whilst the bosses see him as a troublemaker. Owen's isolation is emphasised by the same actors playing his bosses and fellow workers. The men start to come round to Owen's point of view following his simple explanation of 'The Money Trick' – how the capitalist class get richer and richer whilst the working class remain locked in poverty.

Owen has a talent for painting and he is kept on after the refurbishment is complete whilst his fellow workers are laid off. Nonetheless, the annual beano (a kind of picnic) is arranged and a fellow socialist, Barrington, uses this as an opportunity to stand up for his principles in front of his masters. This is followed by 'The Great Oration' in which Barrington sets out the principles of socialism but anyone expecting a happy ending, where the workers overthrow the bosses, is to be disappointed. The socialists do make some progress but it is the bosses that have the final say with their policy of divide and rule.

It wasn't until 1970 that Tressell's grave was identified in a Liverpool cemetery. By that time The Ragged Trousered Philanthropists had already been adapted for the stage and there have been further adaptations since, but I doubt if any are as good as this. I believe that Howard Brenton has produced the definitive stage version.

RAILWAY CHILDREN, THE

Author: E Nesbitt adapted by Mike Kenny
Publisher: Nick Hern Books
ISBN NO: 9781842421318
Cast: 5M 5F + extras
Type: Full length

This play premiered at the National Railway Museum in York before transferring to Platform Twelve of Waterloo Station in London. I don't suppose I'll have much use for that sentence ever again, but you do not need a railway station to stage this play - just imagination.

The story is, of course, about a prosperous Edwardian family brought to near ruin when the father is imprisoned for a crime he did not commit. After moving to a cottage in Yorkshire, the children, Bobbie, Phyllis and Peter spend their time waving at trains that pass them on the way to London in the hope that they will carry their love to their father.

The children's bickering is a delight with Bobbie just about holding everything together with gentle authority. Their pastime of being there to wave every day is rewarded by an old gentleman on the train who waves back. Then, one day, instead of three children he sees only two and they are holding up a sign: "Look out at the station." Mother has fallen ill and the doctor has given them a list of things that are needed. There is no way the children can afford to buy them, so Phyllis meets the old gentleman at the station and gives him the list with a promise that Father will pay him back. The old gentleman provides and Mother recovers.

The audience will be dispersed to the bar with a smile on their lips. As the first act ends with a blockage on the line where the children save the day, Phyllis turns to the audience and says, "I expect some of you are rather disappointed that you didn't see a rail disaster. I would point out that this is supposed to be family entertainment." Like all good family entertainment it has a happy ending. There is always hope and Father is finally re-united with his family.

Anyone familiar with the book or the film will be struck by how faithful this adaptation is to the original, whilst younger members of the audience who do not know the story will be absolutely enthralled by the action. This is, indeed, great family entertainment and Mike Kenny's script provides everything needed for a cracking evening at the theatre.

RED HERRINGS
Author: Steph Deferie
Publisher: www.productionscripts.com
ISBN NO: None
Cast: 3M 3F
Type: Full length

In Red Herrings we are transported to Blue Diamond, a small town outside Las Vegas.

It is 1961 and Madame Lacy Eugenia has a nice little reputation for using her "psychic gift" to help people communicate with their lost loved ones. Sherrif Buckman is convinced she is a fake and that her information comes not from beyond the grave but from his own mother. Nevertheless, she requested to help find the kidnapped grand-baby of a local millionaire. Things start to get complicated when Madame Eugenia's estranged daughter Sophie arrives on the run from her abusive boyfriend Eddie. Then, inevitably, Eddie turns up and things get pretty hot as the characters attempt to out manoeuvre each other, find the baby and claim the reward.

Red Herrings is a clever and funny romp which pays homage to murder mysteries of the fifties and sixties and is great entertainment.

REPLACEMENT, THE
Author: Scott Marshall
Publisher: J Garnett Miller
ISBN NO: 9780853436829
Cast: 2M 1 Voice
Type: One Act

We are apparently in a doctor's surgery where Mr Bonneface has a consultation with the white-coated Salinger. However, some of the questions seem a trifle unusual for a medical consultation: of what relevance can it be that Mr Bonneface holds a heavy goods vehicle licence and supports Accrington Stanley? Their dialogue is intelligent, yet very silly, and there are plenty of laughs to keep us amused as we wonder why the consultation seems to be turning into some sort of audition.

Then, as the characters seem to swap identities, what had been rather Pythonesque becomes quite Beckettian as the tension mounts.

Bonneface becomes threatening but Salinger manages to turn the situation to his own advantage and, when an offstage voice finally explains what it is we have been witnessing, we reach an unexpected though satisfying conclusion.

The Replacement is a challenging piece for two actors but the witty and clever text is bound to please.

REPORT FROM DARKEST UMBRAGE, A
Author: Robert Black
Publisher: www.productionscripts.com
ISBN NO: none
Cast: 2M
Type: Full length

For the second consecutive month I have received a play for review that features Sherlock Holmes. Perhaps Conan-Doyle's stories are undergoing a bit of a revival. This is a very short play featuring Holmes and Watson solving a mystery, involving the apparent murder of a postmistress, merely by reading the reports of the crime in a newspaper.

The author pokes gentle fun at the thought processes employed by Holmes whilst ensuring that all the expected phrases are included in the dialogue. Fun is also had with a young girl at the scene, by the name of Miss Marple, who seems to have better investigative skills than the local police. However the conclusion, that Holmes is prepared to allow the perpetrators of the crime (the theft of Post Office takings) to get away with it because they are nice people,will jar with fans of Conan-Doyle.

RETURN TO VARDIA
Author: Keith Passmore
Publisher: www.productionscripts.com
ISBN NO: none
Cast: 10+M 10+F 10+Other

Return to Vardia is a large cast play for young people set in the Transalvanian Alps. Simon, Ralph and Algie are archaeologists who have lost their camping gear and have no idea how to read a map. On top of that, Algie is seeing shapes in the mist but the three of them have no choice but to find somewhere to shelter for the night. They stumble across a chalice and accidentally summon Marlinus, advisor to the people of Vardia. This is where the story really begins as Marlinus takes the three to a safe place for "food, drink and an interesting story".

There is a multitude of roles to be played in this story of how the people of Vardia fought against the Gorans, who lusted after gold in the mountains, and of the Romans with their thirst for territory, until in the end, good triumphs over evil.

Return to Vardia is indeed an interesting story and, though some of the finer points may be lost on a young audience, it is very suitable for all ages.

REUNION, THE
Author: Peter Gordon
Publisher: Josef Weinberger
ISBN NO: 9780656763359
Cast: 4M 4F
Type: Full length

The Reunion is a play about old friendships and the settling of old scores. Nigel has returned to Yorkshire for a reunion to be held in a rather seedy pub that was once the regular haunt for himself and his mates. Though he didn't order it, there has been a buffet laid on and the play starts with a nice piece of slapstick style action from Jenny, the waitress, which means that an audience will immediately warm to her. As Nigel queries why the buffet has been provided, Jenny assures him that this is the five-fifty a head buffet: you get fancy cut tomatoes for that, but she doesn't mention her own reservations about the sausage rolls.

Peter Gordon has effortlessly, and impressively, set the scene within the first few minutes and we are just getting comfortable when the first twist comes along. Not only did Nigel not order a buffet but now a character, by the name of Mugsy, has turned up to do the disco. In itself, that is not a problem. When you book the function room you get a disco thrown in, but the trouble is that Mugsy is an old acquaintance: one that didn't get invited to the reunion.

The laughs come thick and fast as more characters arrive. Thommo is a dodgy car dealer who arrives with someone who is clearly not his wife. Malcolm is the quiet one of the group who is suddenly saddled with Thommo's lady friend when Mrs Thommo arrives. It soon becomes clear the this reunion is one sausage roll short of a buffet in more ways than one, and when it turns out that Thommo is not the only one who is apparently playing away from home, fists start to fly in a chaotic end to the first act.

Things have calmed down as we enter act two and we now start to learn a little more about the characters. One might expect them to have grown apart over the years but the truth is that they were never very close. Calling themselves the Magnificent Eight, having a secret handshake and an initiation ceremony, is no substitute for making the effort to understand each other and building proper friendships. It is Mugsy, however, who stuns the group with the course his life has taken since they last met.

This is a well constructed and very satisfying play. The characters are realistic and Peter Gordon manages to avoid any clichés as the script takes one or two surprising turns. The Reunion should prove a popular play with many audiences.

ROMEO AND JULIET: PART II
Author: Sandra Hosking
Publisher: www.productionscripts.com
ISBN NO: None
Cast: 2M 1F
Type: One act

Romeo and Juliet: Part II takes as its premise that the star-crossed lovers did not die in that tomb. The dagger has missed its mark and the poison was from a disreputable apothecary and failed to do its duty, and so they lived; but not happily ever after.

Juliet's first line sets the tone: "Romeo! Romeo! Where art thou Romeo? Get your arse in here" and we soon learn that the unfortunate pair have fallen on hard times. He fancies himself as a poet, though he seems more adept at fathering children than producing lines of verse. Juliet has decided that she must go to work if she is to feed the dozen hungry mouths that Romeo has to date provided and declares "Better to be industrious than feeble minded. I'll not dwell in the kitchen as my husband wanders as a feckless fly."

The dialogue throughout is a lot of fun; perhaps not authentic sixteenth century, but it bobs along nicely and is sure to put a smile on the lips of any audience. I felt the storyline got a bit lost for a few pages about two thirds of the way through, but this is a nice one act play which I am sure would do well in a festival.

RUMPLESTILTSKIN
Author: Joy Davis
Publisher: Spotlight Publications
ISBN NO: 9781907307256
Cast: Variable
Type: Pantomime

Outside the castle of Hamalot all the villagers are singing and dancing. A traditional start to a traditional pantomime but with plenty of contemporary references to keep us interested and lots and lots of gloriously silly humour. I loved the very first joke - "I have to put both my babies in one nappy; it's the only way I can make ends meet." - and the laughs just keep coming in the sparkling adaptation of the Brothers Grimm tale.

In his castle King Alfred sits at his square table in despair: not even Laughalot, his jester, can cheer him up. The coffers are empty and the villagers are angry about ever increasing taxes. Where can all the money be going? Then the king hears of a girl called Marigold who has worked out how to turn flax into gold. His troubles are over. Oh no they're not! It is true that she can turn flax into gold but only in the word game where you change one letter at a time. Not realising this, the king throws her into the dungeon and orders her to get to work. Enter one Rumplestiltskin, an evil gnome, who agrees to help Marigold in return for her first born child.

Magically Marigold is freed, she gets to marry a prince and then, after the untimely death of the king – well, quite timely, really, as it happens during the interval – Marigold becomes queen and her noisy first born is the Prince of Wails. Sorry, Wales. Rumplestiltskin appears to claim the child but he is willing to do a deal. If anyone can guess his name then Marigold can keep her baby. Can the Knights of the Square Table save the day? Will one knight, Sir Plus-to-requirements, be the hero? What do you think?

Rumplestiltskin is very funny, a little bit saucy, includes great songs with lyrics adapted to suit the plot and has everything anyone could want from a panto.

SALT

Author: Fiona Peek
Publisher: Nick Hern Books
ISBN NO: 9781848420694
Cast: 2M 2F
Type: Full length

Is it possible to make someone a gift with no strings attached? Is it inevitable that they will feel indebted to you? Can you stop yourself from watching them, ensuring that they use your gift wisely? This is the premise of Salt. The play is described as a modern morality tale about the corrosive effect of money and is the first full length piece from former actor and director Fiona Peek.

All the action takes place around the dinner table in a state-of-the-art kitchen. In an interesting piece of staging, the actors themselves set the props making this part of eachscene. The description of the actors' movements is very precise, leaving little scope for a director to put their own stamp on the production, but there is much comedy in the action as described. The dialogue is fast paced, conversational and, at times, a little obscure. All the characters are quite uninhibited in their use of very strong language and, as we learn more about them, we begin to understand the circumstances that have shaped their personalities.

Things have gone well for Amy and Simon: they have started a family and are financially comfortable. Their good friends Nick and Rachel are not so fortunate. They are childless and they constantly have to rob, or as Nick puts it, 'beat the living shite out of', Peter to pay Paul. They would love to have a child, if only they could, but the cost would be the ruin of them. It therefore goes without saying that it is not long before Rachel reveals that she is pregnant. And so we come to the crux of the story. Amy and Simon cannot stand by and watch their friends go under, so they make them an offer: a gift.

Salt is a very accomplished piece of writing. At times it is funny, at other times, challenging but I fear that the circumscribed nature of the storyline, together with the very strong language could mean that it will have limited appeal within amateur theatre.

SEAGULL
Author: Anton Chekhov
Publisher: Nick Hern Books
ISBN NO: 9781848422100
Cast: 7M 5F
Type: Full Length

The very first production of The Seagull was an unmitigated disaster and the play would have been lost to the world had Constantin Stanislavski not rescued it and turned it into a worldwide hit. The first production in 1896 was marked by the actress playing Nina losing her voice, so intimidated was she by the hostile reaction from the audience. Meanwhile, Chekhov left his seat in the audience and hid behind the scenes for the final two acts. Although it is reported that Chekhov was, himself, unhappy with Stanislavski's production, without it I doubt if audiences would today still be enjoying the genius that is Anton Chekhov.

This new translation is by Charlotte Pyke, John Kerr and Joseph Blatchley. They have meticulously undertaken a word by word translation of the original script, restoring and removing cuts and additions made by the censor prior to that catastrophic first production. A challenge for the translators is to use language understood by a modern audience yet still make it feel 'of the period'. For some reason the phrase 'Annual Leave' seems out of place. I can't recall anyone really using it before the nineteen eighties; it was always just 'holidays' but maybe I've led a sheltered life. Blatchley claims that restoring the words cut by the censor gives depth to the characters and I suppose it is true that we do gain a better understanding of their motivations though I was, in the main, left pondering what the censor found so awful about phrases such as Polina's line, "I have been your wife and friend for twenty years."

However, as this play is, in common with most of Chekhov's writing, more reliant on characterisations than plot, the better we understand their complexities, the better we can enjoy the play. If this new translation results in a few better productions then it has been worth the effort.

SIGNIFICANT OTHERS, THE
Author: John Waterhouse
Publisher: New Playwrights' Network
ISBN NO: 9780863194795
Cast: 4M 2F
Type: One Act

Alan is a worried man. He has had a letter from his parents in Australia to say that they are going to pay him a visit and that they are looking forward to meeting his partner, Sandra. The trouble is that his partner isn't called Sandra – he is called John.

There may have been a time when such a set up would have an audience rolling in the aisles but those days are long gone. This is clearly a very old script which makes the inclusion of references to modern popular culture, such as The Beckhams, seem very odd when the attitudes of the characters are so firmly planted in the nineteen sixties.

Arrangements are made to borrow a woman to pretend to be Sandra, and Alan's parents duly arrive. To everyone's surprise, Sandra is heavily pregnant and, once the stress becomes too much for Alan, he finally tells his parents the truth.

I don't find The Significant Others particularly offensive, it is just very dated and I cannot imagine that it has a place today's theatre.

SWAN, THE
Author: D C Moore
Publisher: Nick Hern Books
ISBN NO: 9781848422193
Cast: 3M 4F
Type: Long One Act

This is the play that accompanies Edgar and Annabel in Double Feature, the first of two volumes published by Nick Hern Books.

The Swan is a pub in Lambeth, London. There is a short prologue set in 1956 then we are in the present day with Jim standing in the doorway, cigarette in mouth, attempting to keep the smoke outside. When it is clear that there is no one around he enters the pub, still smoking, and helps himself to a beer, all the time shouting out good natured threats to the absent landlord.

The Swan is the sort of pub that seldom gets busy, barely surviving due to its inability to attract any passing trade. Today, however, there is a buffet wrapped in clingfilm which Jim barely acknowledges. He sits with his pint and is joined by Russell. With still no sign of the landlord the pair engage in coarse but witty banter and it becomes clear that these men come from very different backgrounds. Jim was virtually born in the pub, whilst Russell chooses it simply because it is the type of place in which his wife would not be seen dead. Speaking of which, the buffet, it transpires, is for a reception following a funeral, possibly the last "do" the pub will host before the developers move in, and there is an awkwardness in the air as both of the men acknowledge that they really ought to be at the service.

Jim is a very engaging character, his use of very strong language disguising an intelligence and charm that make him hard to dislike, even when we learn that his presence in the pub is due to him wishing to avoid the funeral for his own son. As other family members arrive we get a little insight into their complicated lives and how Jim, in his own way, is struggling to keep it together.

All the characters have dialogue that is fresh and free flowing and, though the strong language will put a lot of people off this particular play, D C Moore does demonstrate here a talent that promises much for the future.

THREE-QUARTER MOON
Author: Bryan Darby
Publisher: Jasper Publishing
ISBN NO: 9781906997328
Cast: 3M 3F + 1M with Doubling
Type: Full Length

Three-Quarter Moon is a thriller. The setting is a middle class sitting-cum-dining room with a coffee table set dead centre with an unusual object on it – a heavy looking paperweight about the size of a fist in the shape of a human skull. A potential murder weapon if ever I saw one!

Enter Laura, the lady of the house. She is bustling around preparing for a dinner party and awaiting the arrival of her husband. The front door opens and closes and she calls his name but gets nothing in return except silence. Paperweight at the ready, she prepares herself for an intruder but it turns out to just to be Helen, her neighbour.

The first attempt at humour comes as the pair reminisce about old boyfriends. The he-turned-out-to-be-gay punchline was so obvious I found myself wishing them to just get it over with so that we could return to the plot. Once we do so we learn that Laura is very happily married. She tells Helen that she adores her husband, but that adoration doesn't apparently mean that she trusts him. She is suspicious of him having an affair, her evidence being that, though he often brings gossip home from the office, he has never mentioned his new secretary. So, when he telephones to say that he is leaving immediately to go on a business trip, and Laura believes she hears a voice in the background, her imagination goes into overdrive and she throws the paperweight into the hall in frustration.

Moments later Paul, Laura's husband, staggers in with a head wound explaining that he has been in a car accident. Helen is a nurse and attempts first aid but Paul will have none of it and refuses to go to hospital. When Helen leaves there is a fight and it is Laura that is in need of medical attention.

Red herrings come thick and fast as the story becomes ever more baffling. Helen returns, the dinner guests arrive and then the police turn up investigating Paul's accident. At odds with what we have just seen, the accident happened fifteen miles away and, what is more, both occupants of the car were killed. The significance of the skull shaped paperweight is finally revealed as we enter the world of the supernatural before a final scene that is a repeat of the first one except that it ends differently.

Three-Quarter Moon is a terrifically tangled web of a tale which I fear could confuse audiences into losing track. The story is certainly imaginative but perhaps it has just too many elements.

TONTO EVANS
Author: Frank Vickery
Publisher: Drama Association of Wales
ISBN NO: 9781898740889
Cast: 3M 3F
Type: Full Length

Ray has a dream. It isn't much: all he wants to do is to sit around a camp fire and eat a tin of beans under the stars like the heroes of the Wild West stories that are his passion. But this is a world away from his terraced house in the Welsh valleys where ill health has forced him to sleep downstairs in a bed in the living room. The thing that frustrates him is that now he would be able to afford to go. What was an impossible dream for financial reason is now within his reach if only he was well enough to travel. He has come into eighty thousand pounds and now he broods as his wife, Mair, irons some of the clothes that their son and daughter in law will need for their trip to Disneyland using some of his money!

Later in the day Ray wants to put on his Tonto gear. He used to be an entertainer and his Indian Clobber, as he calls it, earned him a few bob. The visual comedy of Ray dressed head to foot as a Red Indian adds to the humour of the verbal exchanges as he and Mair are at each other hammer and tongs for most of the time. But things suddenly become mysterious. When the son and daughter in law come to collect their ironed clothes they find their father dead on his bed, and mother is nowhere to be found, but a neighbour then reports seeing her hot footing it down the street with a suitcase. The plot thickens when a suicide note is found. The only problem is that the note is in their mother's writing. As the neighbour says, it is like something out of "Linda The Plant" but the mystery unravels when Mair returns. The suicide note turns out to be a list of songs and Ray – well, let's just say all is not as it first appears.

A theme that runs though the script is a reference to a foul smell which I could have done without and another minor quibble is that I feel that some of the stage directions are too descriptive. I accept that sometimes they are important but, most of the time, I believe that the author would have been better leaving it to the director's discretion. However, it doesn't really detract from the fact that Tonto Evans is an enjoyable romp from a writer who clearly knows how to make an audience laugh.

WRITER'S BLOCK
Author: Lauren Dunlop
Publisher: Drama Association of Wales
ISBN NO: 9781898740964
Cast: Min 2M 3F plus 3 Others
Type: One Act

A playwright stares blankly at his laptop. His mind is as empty as the first page of the play he is supposed to be writing. Then he has an idea. How about a stage direction to get him going? Thunder and lightning? A Circus? No? Let's start with the characters, then. At this point a man and woman appear on the stage, completely wooden because the playwright hasn't yet brought them to life.

So begins Writer's Block, a subject that is perhaps dear to Lauren Dunlop's heart and one that has certainly produced a very entertaining little play. The playwright in our story makes the mistake of deciding that his woman should have 'an attitude' and, as a result, things soon spiral out of his control. Things don't quite go the way the heroine had imagined, however, as her dreams are spoilt by the villain of the piece being, well, villainous.

Writer's Block is clever and funny and something that will be enjoyed by cast and audience alike. With the villain being the only British character it should do well in the American market but there is no reason why it shouldn't also be enjoyed on the British stage.

PLAYS BY DAVID MUNCASTER

Published by New Theatre Publications
www.plays4theatre.com

CALL GIRLS
One Act - Comedy. 1m 4f

Call Girls is set in a call centre providing IT assistance to an
unspecified company. Three of the women get on well together and
'have a laugh' but for the last six months their happy little group
has been spoiled by the presence of Laura, an arrogant and aloof
troublemaker whose predilection for short skirts and low cut tops
probably has more to do with her getting the job than any particular
work skills. Thankfully this is Laura's last week and the others decide
not to let her go without letting her know exactly what they think of
her. Surprisingly it is Mary, normally the quietest member of the group,
who really lets rip but this uncharacteristic outburst could be the
biggest mistake of her life.

COMMUNITY SPIRIT
Full length - Farce. 8m 3f

The village of Snickerton has a new community hall and all the local
groups get together to organise an opening day that will never be
forgotten. Pity Mel, the poor official from the local council who has to
try to keep apart the warring factions. There is Mike, the bombastic
chairman from the choral society, who clashes with Chris, his deadly
rival, as well as just about anyone else who dare to disagree with him.
Add a couple of luvies from the am dram, some representatives of
Churches Together who couldn't be further apart, the leader of the
cubs and beavers who sees things in the night, and a host of other
characters including a caretaker with a very unfortunate name.
Community Spirit is a large cast play with eleven speaking roles and
any number of none speaking roles that starts out as a comedy of
manners but by the end is pure farce. Great fun for any theatre group
looking to involve as many of their members as possible

FRESH SHOWERS FOR THE THIRSTING FLOWERS
One Act Play 2f

Alice is a retired English teacher who is living a comfortable if rather lonely existence. A chance encounter with her neighbour's daughter re-awakens her passion to teach when she discovers that most unusual of things. A pupil who wants to learn! With a respectful nod to 'Educating Rita' this is a story of how a generation gap is easily bridged through the discovery of a mutual interest. All scenes are set in Alice`s living room which has minimal set requirements. The title of this play is taken from the poem 'The Cloud' by Percy Bysshe Shelley. Other quotes in this play are considered 'fair usage' and do not contravene copyright law but a licence is required to use the music specified.

MAD GARY'S FRUIT AND NUT CASE
Full length - Comedy Thriller. 4m 4f

It is a big day for Tommy. His lovely daughter Peaches has just married Lionel Looselips, the son of the biggest fruit and veg wholesale magnate in the whole of the county. Now Tommy can be assured that his market stall will always have the freshest, best value produce known to man. The wedding reception is a grand affair, friends and relations are joined by rivals who, for one day, put their differences aside; or do they? As the ceremonial fruit salad is consumed the guests start dropping like fruit flies. Who is responsible for this murderous act? What did they hope to gain? Who will be next? It's a job for "Mad" Gary Grasslover of the local constabulary.

This intentionally corny and ribald comedy/murder mystery provides plenty of laughs and opportunity for the audience to join in the fun by, not only trying to guess the murderer, but also by selected members being given characters to play.

MISSION IMPOSSIBLE
One Act - Comedy. 2m 3f

A meeting room, a flip chart, an enthusiastic facilitator, and four employees who are determined to give her a hard time. This is the background to Mission Impossible, a hilarious look at the corporate nonsense that anyone who has ever attended a team bonding session will know only too well. Ice Breakers and silly games do little to bond this team as the beleaguered facilitator gets tough to ensure that she gets the outcome she desires. Mission Impossible won the Congleton One Act Play Festival 2009.

WAITING FOR A TRAIN
Full length. 4f

Set on the platform of a rural railway station waiting for a train that never comes, this is a play about life, love and hope. The stark reality of living with schizophrenia is contrasted by the warmth and playfulness that exists between the main characters. With a degree of flexibility in casting and a set that would work better if it is suggested rather than detailed this is play should be relatively simple to stage at the same time giving the actors the opportunity to immerse themselves into characters that have great complexity and depth.

Published by YouthPlays
www.youthplays.com

THE KENNEL CLUB
One act - Comedy. 2m 2f

The Kennel Club is a short play set in rescue kennels. The four characters are dogs. Sally, the sensible Golden Retriever, Molly her nervous partner, Sam, a scatterbrained terrier and Bruno, the huge monster with a heart of gold. These diverse characters are all going to have to work together if Sally's plan to find them all new homes is going to work. The Kennel Club is a touching and funny short play that has won festivals on both sides of the Atlantic and is popular with both children and adults.

THE PUBLISHERS

Samuel French Ltd
52 Fitzroy Street
London W1T 5JR
P: 02073879373
W: www.samuelfrench-london.co.uk

Josef Weinberger
12-14 Mortimer Street
London W1T 3JJ
P: 020 75802827
W: www.josef-weinberger.co.uk

Stagescripts
Lantern House
84 Littlehaven Lane
Horsham
West Sussex
RH12 4JB
P: 0845 686 0611
W: www.stagescripts.com

New Theatre Publications
2 Hereford Close
Woolston
Warrington
Cheshire
WA1 4HR
P: 01925 485605
W: www.plays4theatre.com

Spotlight Publications
259 The Moorings
Dalgety Bay
Fife KY11 9GX
P: 01383 825 737
W: www.spotlightpublications.com

Cressrelles Publishing
10 Station Road Industrial Estate
Colwall
Herefordshire
WR13 6RN
P: (01684) 540 154
W: www.cressrelles.co.uk

Nick Hern Books
The Glasshouse
49a Goldhawk Road
London
W12 8QP
P: 0208 749 4953
W: www.nickhernbooks.co.uk

Oberon Books
521 Caledonian Road
London N7 9RH
P: 02076073637
W: www.oberonbooks.com

Lazy Bee Scripts
2 Wood Road
Ashurst
Southampton
SO40 7BD
P: 023 8029 3120
W: www.lazybeescripts.co.uk

All plays in this volume can be purchased via
www.amateurstagemagazine.co.uk

The only monthly magazine passionate about amateur theatre

www.ingramcontent.com/pod-product-compliance
Lightning Source LLC
La Vergne TN
LVHW021517080426
835509LV00018B/2549